Towards a New Economic Order

Europe and the International Order

Series Editor: Joel Krieger

The dramatic events of 1989, perestroika and the ultimate collapse of the Soviet Union, the end of the Cold War, European integration, and the aftermath of the War in the Persian Gulf mark a period of extraordinary volatility in Europe. This series considers the causes, dimensions, and consequences of these new transitions in European politics. It includes books which transcend the divisions of East and West, challenge narrow disciplinary approaches, and examine the connections between international and domestic politics.

Published

Forthcoming

Towards a New Economic Order
Postfordism, Ecology and Democracy

ALAIN LIPIETZ

Translated by
Malcolm Slater

Polity Press

First published in France as *Choisir L'Audace*, copyright © Éditions La
Découverte, 1989
This English translation copyright © Polity Press 1992
Preface and Postscript to this edition © Polity Press 1992
Published with the assistance of the French Ministry of Culture

First published in 1992 by Polity Press
in association with Blackwell Publishers

Editorial office:
Polity Press
65 Bridge Street
Cambridge CB2 1UR, UK

Marketing and production:
Blackwell Publishers
108 Cowley Road
Oxford OX4 1JF, UK

ISBN 0 7456 0865-5
ISBN 0 7456 0866-3 (pbk)

A CIP catalogue record for this book is available
from the British Library.

Typeset in 11 on 13 pt Times
by Best-set Typesetter Ltd., Hong Kong
Printed in Great Britain by T.J. Press Ltd, Padstow, Cornwall.

This book is printed on acid-free paper.

Contents

Preface to the English Edition

In 1981 a coalition of the Socialist and Communist Parties came to power in France, led by President François Mitterrand and bearing the hopes of French 'people of the left'. However, its policies very soon came up against the economic crisis and constraints imposed on France by the institutions of the European Economic Community. In March 1983, faced with a worsening trade deficit and intractable unemployment, the left-wing government in France abandoned its aim of social reforms, which were sacrificed to the competitiveness of French firms.

At the time, I was an economist committed to the left, though since 1968 I had opposed the statist and productivist policies of the left in France. The year 1984 saw the publication of my book *L'Audace ou l'enlisement – sur les politiques économiques de la gauche* (Paris, La Découverte). In it I explained the reasons for the 1981–3 failure, but I also criticized the capitulation of March 1983 and proposed a 'different policy'. The book made a great impact and I was invited to give over a hundred lectures and radio broadcasts . . . but the government, now minus the Communists, pursued a policy which was more and more economically neo-liberal and politically repressive.

The 1986 National Assembly elections were won by the right, which hastened the move to neo-liberalism. In 1988, François Mitterrand was re-elected president and fresh legislative elections brought back the Socialist Party, which maintained a neo-liberal economic policy. The result was that unemployment worsened in France throughout the 1980s and social inequalities increased enormously.

Against this background of social degradation, with all hopes of change gone, the racist extreme right (Jean-Marie Le Pen's National Front Party) began to flourish, gaining 10 per cent of votes in the 1984 European Parliament elections and 15 per cent in the 1988 presidential elections.

For me, it was clear that the left in France no longer offered an alternative – neither the Socialist Party, transformed into a mere manager of capitalist interests, nor the Communist Party, bogged down in a productivist and statist ideology, unable to make the break with Stalinism. In the 1986 National Assembly elections, I headed the list of ecologists and 'alternatives' in the working-class area of Seine-Saint-Denis, just outside Paris. Our vote, like that of nearly all ecologists, was very low – 3 per cent. Nevertheless, in 1988 I joined the Green Party, at the same time continuing to write on the crisis and possible solutions to it, particularly in the Third World.[1]

The year 1989 promised to be a crucial one, with local council and European Parliament elections. I therefore wrote this book of *proposals*, as a non-academic contribution to Green thinking on economic matters. The Greens made spectacular election gains – more than 20 per cent of votes in some cities, and 11 per cent in the European elections, giving them 9 out of the 81 French members of the European Parliament. Unfortunately, the National Front gained slightly more, with the Socialist Party on 22 per cent and the Communists on 7 per cent. In the 1992 regional elections however, the ecologists, with 14 per cent of total votes, came out slightly ahead of the National Front; I was elected regional councillor after a campaign in which the economic policies of the Greens, very close to my proposals in this book, were widely reported in the press.

In the 1990s, political ecology, represented by a 39-

strong Green Group in the European Parliament, is playing an increasing role in a Western Europe which has gone down the road of greater unity. However, since the publication in early 1989 of the French edition, Europe has experienced a further spectacular change: the aim at the end of the book – the liberation of Eastern Europe – became reality at the end of 1989. Yet if Europe proved powerless when it came to the first crisis of the new era – the second Gulf War, it had rather more clout at the United Nations 1992 Rio Conference on the Environment and Development.

I do not go back on anything I proposed for Eastern Europe in the final chapter – on the contrary! However, I have added a postscript to update the book in the light of the new situation. I have omitted only what would not be understood by the non-French reader.

I warmly thank my translator, who patiently adapted a book originally destined for a wide French readership. My conviction is that this book is more than an analysis of progressist French thinking; it is a contribution to debates by social movements determined to change the world to save it from the catastrophes which threaten it, in East and West, and North and South.

Alain Lipietz

The extract on pp. 49–50 from Sophocles' Antigone *is reproduced by permission of Penguin Books Ltd from Sophocles*, The Theban Plays, *trans. E. F. Watling, © E. F. Watling, 1947.*

Introduction

All too often, economists treat their subject (societies based on markets and wage-labour) as if it could be defined by immutable laws, behaviour and tendencies. This is certainly true for the kind of economics which wins Nobel prizes – the kind which claims that there is a form of organization which, though not yet perfect, has already been broadly established, and ensures that wealth is generated and distributed with optimal efficiency. This form of economic organization is, of course, our own! But it is also too often true of Marxist economists, who say that there have been – and will be – other modes of production but that, in between the massive ruptures introduced by revolutions, modes of production (capitalism, in particular) can be seen as essentially unchanging. Only the transition to socialism would really allow us to 'change the logic of economic action', as if leaving Babylon to found the new Jerusalem.

The best economists, of course, Marxist or otherwise, have highlighted changes in the economic system, from the gradual to the cataclysmic, during its long history. But they, or their followers, tend to reduce these changes to a quantitative evolution which conforms to the 'overall logic of the system': increasing mechanization, further concentration of property, and so on.

We are nowadays aware that history is much more complex, contingent and fluid. Since 1848 (the year of the *Communist Manifesto* and of the last great 'subsistence crisis' of the economic *ancien régime*), capitalism has undergone more significant changes than any socialist thinker of the time could have imagined. Changes more profound even than those expected from the transition to socialism! Throughout this process, enormous social tensions and major economic problems built up, leading to crises, political struggle, wars and (sometimes) political revolutions. But these revolutions, even so-called 'socialist' ones, have not so far led to fundamentally different forms of economic organization and, faced with their own distinctive problems, they now appear to be falling into line with the age-old rules of capitalism: markets and profits.

Despite this turbulent history, capitalism seems to function in a reasonably stable way over long periods. Even in times of conflict and recession, its overall framework, its aims and rules are by and large accepted by almost everyone. This framework and these aims and rules have been thrown into turmoil three times in the course of history: at the end of the nineteenth century, in the 1930s–50s and since the end of the 1960s. But in the intervals between these major crises, there was a 'grand compromise' between social groups, the basis of which was a 'development model' consisting of a definition, adopted for the time being, of what humanity can best expect from economic activity: the organizing principles of the labour process, the aims of production and the ground rules for resolving tensions.

This development model is itself enveloped in a broader 'world view', including a definition of the benefits of living in society: these are the cement of the Grand Compromise, which can then be defended by the whole political spectrum, from right to left. There are arguments about sectional interests and about improvements to the model on the basis of the same world view. But the model itself, the overall design, is not challenged: we accept the promises of the model as a practical ideal, as the aim of our social activity, whether economic or political. In these periods, utopias offering change exist, but they are far removed from the everyday ('reformist', if you will) practice of those who advocate them.

In a 'major crisis', the situation is quite different. On these occasions, the model and its aims, rules and promises seem out of date: unworkable economically and rejected politically and socially. These periods are the crossroads of history, when initiatives for change override the dead weight of routine; they are open periods, where the out-come remains uncertain for well over a decade – periods when blueprints or 'projects' are redefined, and social forces realigned. An example occurred in the 1930s–50s, when social democracy and Rooseveltism threw down the challenge to free-market conservatism, itself in crisis and in mortal combat with Fascism and Stalinism.

We are today, and have been for twenty years, in one of those open periods when what is in contention is not the fairest and most efficient way to apply an agreed model, but the actual definition of a new development model, a new grand compromise. We are not only in an economic crisis, but in a crisis of the compromise on which our society is based, a crisis of the 'project'. This situation is sometimes called a 'crisis of hegemony'; that is, of the ability of elites and the social groups which sustain them to offer a world view and a development model acceptable to society as a whole.

In this book, we will first summarize the post-war 'hegemonic' development model and the reasons why it has been thrown into crisis. Firstly, because the questions raised by this crisis ('What has gone wrong?') are addressed by any project offering a 'way out of the crisis'. Even if the responses differ, they must (at least) address this list of questions. Secondly, because it will allow us to identify what a development model needs for it to 'stand up'.

We will then look at the strengths and weaknesses

of what was offered in the 1980s as the main candidate to provide a new development model, which I shall call 'productivist liberalism'. Even though by the end of the 1980s it was not making much progress, even though its champions (in the United States and Britain) are running into difficulties, and even though some limited versions of a different model are gaining ground, it still represents the 'main enemy' for those who do not share its underlying world view. Finally, I shall put forward another development model, based on a different world view. Or, more modestly, elements of a possible post-crisis grand compromise – an alternative for the twenty-first century, or even for the 1990s.

But it must be stressed that although the world view consonant with a development model which has achieved hegemony is supported by the stability and advantages of that model (so that it comes to be regarded as natural), the world view corresponding to an unstabilized, unrealized model is only ever a *project*. It cannot be derived from any historical law, let alone an economic one. Just as the popularized variants of Marxism, offering a glorious future as an inevitable consequence of the development of productive forces and the dialectical laws of historical materialism, were misleading, so too are current ideologies (sustained by the same productivist, technocratic mixture) which, while promising us 'an end to ideologies', claim to predict how future society will develop from the characteristics of the present 'technological revolution'.

Clearly, the alternative project would simply be another distant revolutionary utopia (though extremely valuable, like a compass showing the North Pole for a boat sailing north from Corsica to Marseilles) if it did not build on aspirations and behaviour already present in the real world. As an outline of a future grand compromise, it would need to take account of the rules of thumb, experiences and achievements – already crowned by success in some countries – of certain sections of the dominant classes. Like any world view (the more pedantic but more precise term 'societal paradigm' will be used later), the alternative, if it becomes hegemonic, will have its 'right' and 'left'. It will have an employers' version – in fact this already exists! Let us not complain that it has been 'taken over by the other side': if one wants a project to become dominant, one must accept that others will take it over, distort and disfigure it; but it also means making others accept one's own values (even reluctantly and in diluted form): it means making them accept a more advanced compromise.

Before being 'taken over', a new project comes up against resistance – not only from the old model on the way out, but also from others offering different answers to the same questions, or even avoiding certain questions. They offer answers which proponents of the alternative project consider unacceptable and inhuman, but which, unfortunately, are feasible, and already in place, just as Fascism was a response to questions posed by anarchy in the market and the crisis of overproduction of liberal capitalism. It was a 'solution' which at times tied in with the preoccupations of social democrats, Communists or Roosevelt. Nevertheless, it took World War II, a veritable civil war on a world scale, to stabilize the social democratic compromise and to start the movement towards colonial independence. Was this mere reformism? Were the hopes of the wartime resistance being exploited for other ends? Probably, but such developments were preferable to the victory of the other 'solutions'.

When I talk of the alternative, therefore, my starting point will of course be the world view which is gradually emerging from practice and from the hopes of movements termed 'alternative' in Europe and 'radical' in the United States, and from new trends in the trade union movement, ecology and feminism. But at the same time I shall bear in mind that it also exists, in a weakened form, in certain industrial or institutional compromises already in being; and that, in both its radical and its moderate versions, it has to contend with something much more powerful – liberal productivism, even though this is undermined by already glaring contradictions.

As Marx said, 'Men make their own history, but they do so on the basis of existing conditions, inherited from the past.'

1
The Fordist Compromise

To understand the present crisis, we must understand the dominant thinking of the post-war period. The prolonged boom of this era (Jean Fourastié spoke of 'thirty glorious years') amounted to a real golden age of capitalism. More significantly, the workers' movement, and its parties and labour unions, seems even today to regard it as a bygone golden age – not a paradise, but at least one of the ways, perhaps *the* way, to paradise – whose achievements, it is claimed, were undone by the crisis. This shows that the development model which fashioned this period was indeed 'hegemonic', in that it inspired a world view shared by left and right.

This of course was true only of developed capitalist countries, even though the ideal of most elites in 'under-developed' countries was to 'catch up with' this model, by some means or other. We need to distinguish, therefore, between the development model as applied in nation-states (developed capitalist ones, that is), and the global order or 'international configuration' which makes these national compromises possible, at the same time as reflecting their success in a limited number of countries.

What is a development model?

As applied at national level to countries where it is dominant, a development model consists of three legs of a tripod, and can be analysed from three points of view:

• *A labour process model* (or 'technological paradigm' or 'industrialization model', depending on the writer, and from slightly different perspectives). This involves the general principles governing the labour process and the way it evolves during the period when the model is dominant. These principles cover not only how the labour process is organized within firms, but also the division of labour between firms. There may be, of course, whole sectors or regions which remain outside the model, but it remains a 'model' in that the most 'advanced' sectors in terms of these principles determine how others will evolve.

• *A regime of accumulation.* The logic and laws of macro-economics describe the parallel development, over a long period, of the conditions of production on the one hand (productivity of labour, degree of mechanization, relative importance of the various branches of production) and, on the other hand, the conditions under which production is put to social use (household consumption, investment, government spending, foreign trade).

• *A mode of regulation.* This involves all the mechanisms which adjust the contradictory and conflictual behaviour of individuals to the collective principles of the regime of accumulation. At the basic level, these means of adjustment are simply the extent to which entrepreneurs and workers are in the habit of conforming, or are willing to conform, to these principles, because they recognize them (even reluctantly) as valid or logical. At another level, institutionalized forms are more important – the rules of the market, social welfare provision, money, financial networks. These institutionalized forms can be state-determined (laws, executive acts, public finances), private (collective agreements) or semi-public (a social security system such as the French one).

In this way, a regime of accumulation is the macro-economic result of the way the mode of regulation functions, with a labour process model as its basis. It is the whole of this which constitutes a 'development model' – but it is only *a* model, and not of *all* development, since it is wrong to speak of 'obstacles to development' or 'the end of development', as if development was a fixed route, a long road down which different peoples go, like a cycle race with breakaway riders, a main bunch and inevitable stragglers.

Of course, at any one time, there will be a 'leading group' which has defined and imposed its view of how to proceed. But a development model holds good only as long as its promises coincide with a certain possible conception of happiness. This idea of happiness may collapse, either when it is clear that the model can no longer guarantee it, or when the disadvantages of the model are more and more glaring. Nations then enter a period of searching, of hesitation (when monstrosities can proliferate!). Social and political conflicts, in work situations, in everyday life, in the state, lead to the gradual emergence of the conditions for a new 'tripod'. The extra-economic conditions for the stability of this 'tripod' will be examined later. For now, we will look at the characteristics of the post-war tripod, which some French theorists (taking their lead from pre-war writers such as Gramsci, the Italian Marxist, and Henri de Man, the Belgian corporatist) have called 'Fordism'.

Fordism[1]

The Fordist labour process model involved the conjunction of Taylorism and mechanization within large, multi-department firms, which subcontracted certain tasks to other firms following the same principles. It is by looking at Taylorism in particular that an understanding of the current crisis can be reached.

Taylorism can be seen as the *rationalization* of production, based on an increasing separation of the 'ideas people' and organizers of production (engineers, and organization and maintenance staff) and the 'operatives' carrying out production – semi-skilled manual workers performing repetitive tasks. This did not mean that the operatives 'had no need to think', that the mental and manual aspects of work were completely separate (even though Taylor did say this and people have too often repeated it since). In fact, even in the most robotized textile factory, an operative *does* have to think about the task in hand, if only to avoid injury or stop a thread jumping. But this conscious *'involvement'* (a word which will occur many times in this book!) has to remain 'informal', 'hidden' and even 'paradoxical' – the engineer or the supervisor will deny that the operative has to think, and will simply give the order to follow the correct drill . . . but they are counting on the operative's initiative to make sure all goes well. The operative tries hard to make sure all goes well, thereby asserting the autonomy of a thinking being . . . in the service of those specialized in mental labour. This skill cannot be systematized and collectivized, however, unlike the old craft skills (still surviving in watchmaking and construction) which were passed on from 'master' to 'craftsman'.

When Taylor and his followers introduced these principles at the beginning of the twentieth century, the aim was in fact to generalize the 'best practice' of craft and specialist workers, while depriving them of the prime position which their monopoly of skills gave them in the workplace. Their supremacy had been concretized in customs, privileges, a steady workrate and other microcompromises at workshop level. The first three decades of this century witnessed the stubborn resistance – and the defeat – of these workers with specialized skills, and their acceptance (even by Communist labour unions) of the new compromise. In exchange for Taylorist forms of control, the unions asked for a share of the productivity gains accruing from rationalization.

This grand compromise (sharing productivity gains) was at first accepted by only a small minority of employers – such as Henry Ford of Model T fame – and bankers and politicians, such as John Maynard Keynes. Ford and Keynes were aware that increased productivity gains from the Taylorist revolution would lead to a massive crisis of overproduction if there was no corresponding revolution on the demand side. And what could be a more powerful factor in the growth of demand for firms' goods than a steady growth in the real wages of the workers themselves?

But the words of Ford and Keynes fell on deaf ears. The only thing which could force all bosses to increase simultaneously the purchasing power of their workers was pressure from the unions, which they were striving to suppress, and whose successes had to be won locally, firm by firm. Employers found it easier to treat their employees as producers to be coerced rather than as a crop of consumers. The fears of Ford, Keynes and the labour unions, faced with the free-market conservatism of Hoover, Lloyd George or Laval, were realized in the disasters of the 1930s Great Depression, a gigantic crisis of overproduction.

In fact, to solve this thorny problem of how to organize social demand beyond competition between firms, there were three competing alternatives to free-market conservatism (with connections between them, used by theorists, politicians and even unions): Fascism, Stalinism – both in favour of the state organization of demand, but disagreeing strongly about the goals to which it should be directed – and social democracy, a 'left' version of what Keynes and Ford were proposing 'from the right'; that is, an organized, all-embracing compromise between employers and unions to redistribute productivity gains to workers.

Fortunately, Fascism was defeated in World War II by a coalition of the others; and, in less than ten years, the struggle between Stalinism and what we will call the Fordist compromise was won by the latter. This compromise took shape as a regime of accumulation and a mode of regulation.

The regime of accumulation can be described as:

● mass production, involving growing polarization between skilled mental labourers and deskilled operatives, and increasing mechanization leading to a sharp rise in productivity and an increase in the volume of capital goods per worker;
● a proportionate share-out of value added; that is, increased real wages to match increases in productivity;
● a consequent stability in firms' profitability, with plant used at full capacity, and full employment.

In other words, the Fordist compromise matched greater mass production with higher mass consumption. It became known throughout the world after the war as the 'American way of life' – a productivist model which was 'hedonist' in that it was based on the pursuit of happiness through the mass availability of a greater number of goods. The only people to voice their opposition were a few intellectuals, like Herbert Marcuse. This concept of progress and the pursuit of happiness was regarded as a goal by a whole spectrum of political movements, ranging from Conservatism through Christian Democracy and socialism to Communism. Even Conservative parties overcame the resistance of those employers who saw their short-term interest only in terms of reducing wages.

Such employers had to be forced to adhere to the principles of the compromise, which in any case corresponded to their medium-term interests; and this was done by modes of regulation established after the war, which, despite differences between countries, all had the following ingredients:

- social legislation covering minimum wage levels and generalized collective agreements, which made employers give their workers annual wage rises in line with increased national productivity;
- a 'welfare state'; that is, an advanced system of social security which meant that wage-earners (indeed, the whole population) remained consumers even when they were prevented from 'earning their living' through illness, retirement, unemployment or the like.
- credit money (that is, pure paper money) issued by private banks, though controlled by central banks, as the economy demanded and not as a function of available gold reserves.

All these institutions offered a new framework, a new set of ground rules. They conferred on the state an active responsibility for controlling the economy; through budget deficits, or government spending, it could stimulate growth. As overseer of the banking system, it could ease or restrict credit and thereby boost or slow down investment by firms and individuals. The use of these 'levers' was dubbed 'Keynesian policy'.

However, this new role did not necessarily mean, in the United States, for example, or even in Sweden, more public ownership of production, though this did happen in France and Italy. Moreover, nationalization in the legal sense does not imply a change in social relationships. Renault workers were aware of this from the start: whether their employer was public or private, Taylorism prevailed.

Another big mistake is to think that the network of regulatory devices was instituted *with the intention* of making Fordism work, though with hindsight, I have presented it as if it was. However, collective agreements and social security were not achieved by Fordism, but by workers, earned by the blood shed at Adalen in Sweden, the struggles of the new CIO labour union under Roosevelt, the blood of French and Italian resistance fighters, or the tenacity of the British working class during the Blitz. These were achievements which the victors passed on to Japan and Germany, to prevent resurgence of the military-industrial bloc. Fordism grew out of the coincidence of this social pressure with the thinking of a small number of employers, and those who theorized about this coincidence (Beveridge in Great Britain, Pierre Massé or Bloch-Lainé in France) were not the creators of it, even though they were often the architects of its institutionalization.

The new mode of regulation, appropriate for a new development model, arose from national social struggles within the wider context of a fierce worldwide contest with Fascist and Stalinist models. This is why the regulatory institutions developed to a varying degree in different countries. For example, after the war and the Roosevelt era, the United States took a great leap backwards with the Cold War and McCarthyism. Even the reforms of Kennedy and Johnson (attacked by Reagan in the 1980s) did not give the American people a social security system like those in Northern Europe. In France, Fordism reached its apotheosis only with the Grenelle agreements of June 1968, which put an end to the 'May events' – perhaps the first great anti-Fordist mass movement!

History has a devious nature: we need to remember this experience in any current analysis of the way solutions to the present crisis are emerging.

American hegemony

At the international level, the world economy has never reached an equivalent degree of organized regulation, negotiated between 'partners'. To begin with, the Fordist model came to dominate only OECD countries, if one excepts Turkey and includes Finland, though the latter before the war was among the 'less advanced countries'. Most Third World countries were excluded (or excluded themselves – the question will not be discussed here), and were therefore marginalized, in the 1950s, as far as trade in industrial goods was concerned. Semi-free trade grew up between the Fordist countries, and their biggest markets were each other. Trade in industrial goods grew rapidly, raising questions about the regulation of world trade and particularly about an international currency. The response was the *de facto* acceptance of the dollar as the international credit currency, and the management of trade balances by changes in parity and by national policies to 'damp down' domestic markets.

The dollar's privileged position was made possible because the United States had the best labour process model (industrial *and* agricultural). American goods were both highly competitive and, until the middle of the 1950s, indispensable. The dollar was therefore accepted for international payments by all other countries, who were always in need of US currency. It was a period when, since the US trade balance (the difference between exports and imports) was structurally in surplus, its balance of payments could be structurally in deficit. In other words, it was possible for the outward flow of dollars for investment or military spending abroad to be permanently larger than the inward flow to buy goods. The United States therefore gave to Japan and Western Europe, in the form of technology or capital transfers (such as the Marshall Plan), the means to catch up; in exchange, for the price of the paper money it printed, it acquired part of its allies' production.

What needs to be emphasized is the similarity between this American approach – an attitude of undiluted hegemony, or of 'leadership' as the Americans would say – and the Fordist compromise within a country. Just as employers had to grant wage increases to keep the working class away from Communism and create an army of consumers, so the American elites and the administration in the end resisted the temptation to crush possible competitors and reduce Europe and Japan to the level of underdeveloped countries by flooding them, through relentless free trade, with their own goods. On the contrary, after 1947 they made up European and Japanese deficits by multifaceted 'aid'. They did not prevent their new allies from indulging in protectionism and consolidating their currencies. They accepted discrimination against themselves in their trade relations with them. They financed the reconstruction of their competitors' industry and future exporting capacity. The aim of this 'altruism' was to reinstate markets which were prosperous and above all anti-Communist.

In the Third World, on the other hand, the pursuit of short-term interests led them to frustrate the desire for independent development, despite the 'Alliance for Progress' advocated by a few 'liberals' and tried out by Kennedy. There was no Marshall Plan for the Third World, merely a terrible catalogue of murders of nationalist leaders, absurd embargoes, engineered coups d'état, support for the most sordid dictatorships, neo-colonial wars and 'minor tragedies'.

The Fordist world view

We can now look again at the characteristics of the 'world view' central to the Fordist compromise, or, as I called it earlier, its 'societal paradigm'. 'Paradigm', from the Greek word meaning 'model', 'example', 'emblem', is a term used mainly in grammar to describe words or phrases which can be replaced by others of the same kind. For example, in the phrase 'I have a blue pen', the word 'blue' can be replaced by another colour adjective; this is the paradigm of colours. But 'I have a walk pen' is wrong: we have gone outside the paradigm. 'Paradigm' therefore conveys the idea of a 'common core' which accepts variants, but within certain limits. The world view which permeates a certain era and shapes agreement on a certain way of life in society, on the basis of a particular conception of what is moral and normal and desirable, constitutes a 'societal paradigm', which duplicates, at the level of ideas and behaviour, the development model.

A simplified description of the foundations of the Fordist paradigm would be as follows:

● The organization of production is best restricted to dominant groups (employers, technocrats), by extension of the Taylorist industrial model, which denies mere 'operatives' any intellectual involvement in the labour process.
● Wage-earners and indeed the whole population will, in the normal course of things, recoup some of the productivity gains through a set of legislative or contractual forms of regulation, in such a way that, as purchasing power increases with productivity, full employment is virtually assured.
● People should receive this directly through wages or through the welfare state; but in any case in the form of money giving access to traded goods and services.
● Full employment and the advance of mass consumption are the goals of technical progress and economic growth, and the state's role is to make sure these are achieved.

In other words, the Fordist paradigm offers a three-pronged conception of progress: technical progress (meaning technological progress, driven forwards unfettered by 'intellectual workers'), social progress (meaning greater purchasing power and a greater scope for consumer goods), and the progress of the state (meaning defence of the general interest against 'encroachments' by individual interests). Such a conception of progress gives precedence to 'hierarchy' (or organization) rather than to the market; it is 'organicist' in that theoretically it denies nobody 'a share in the fruits of progress', though in practice there will always be people who are excluded. On the other hand, as a matter of course, it does exclude unskilled production workers from control over their activities, and ordinary citizens from decisions about what constitutes progress in terms of consumption, public services, urban planning, and more generally anything involving the ecological consequences of 'progress'. It also means that solidarity itself, organized by the welfare state, takes on an exclusively administrative form.

Under pressure from followers of Roosevelt and social democrats, this paradigm became dominant after 1945 in advanced capitalist countries, following the defeat of the Fascist alternative to classical liberalism; it was also in competition with the Soviet alternative. However, since it could be managed by conservative political forces or Christian democrats as well as by social democrats, with or without Communist support, it constituted a 'hegemonic paradigm' dominating everybody, even though it was rightly called 'social democrat'.

This compromise was hit by crisis from all sides at once: the lower profitability of the Fordist productive model, the internationalization of markets and production which compromised national regulation, workers turning against it because of alienation from work and because of the omnipotence of hierarchy and the state, citizens wanting more autonomy, and growing reservations about 'administrative' solidarity.

The French left's 'Joint Programme' of 1972, signed by the Socialist Party, the Communist Party and a small centre-left party, can be regarded as a radicalized culmination of the Fordist compromise. The French left which, during the Liberation and the Fourth Republic, and even in opposition under Gaullism,[2] had contributed greatly to the consolidation of this model, can be seen as 'the left of the Fordist compromise'.

It is no accident that, in May 1968, the massive youth and workers' movement largely escaped the left's control, and was often as hostile to it as to the Gaullist regime. The May 1968 movement was the first mass revolt against the Fordist paradigm. It was brought to a halt by the Grenelle agreements of June 1968, when the unions obtained a huge increase in 'social advantages' within Fordism, in return for ending the biggest strike in history – nine million people were on strike for three weeks. All subsequent anti-Fordist social movements – ecologists, regionalists, feminists – had their beginnings outside the traditional left. But in the 1970s, economic crisis and a series of setbacks led the 'people of '68' gradually, if reluctantly, back to the parties of the Joint Programme (particularly the Socialist Party). These were seen, at least in part, as offering a political outlet for their aspirations, and in any event as the proponents of a non-reactionary way out of the crisis.

Unfortunately, when the left-wing parties which were the vehicle of this vision of progress came to power in 1981, the material foundations of their hopes had evaporated. The Fordist development model was in terminal decline.

2
The End of the Golden Age

The great Fordist compromise and the virtuous world order dominated by the United States began to break up towards the end of the 1960s – because of two chains of events. The first one can be understood in a national context, taking each country as if it were an isolated planet: the crisis of the model itself. The second factor of disintegration was international, arising from the increasing interpenetration of national economies. Naturally, an analysis of what happened has to look at the way these two sets of events overlapped, but, to understand clearly the problems facing us, it is easier to look at them separately, beginning with the internal causes.[1]

The crisis of Fordism

In the second half of the glorious decade of the 1960s – though it emerged only later, when the statistics were available – productivity gains began to fall off in most branches of industrial activity in developed capitalist countries. Nevertheless, not only did increases in real wages continue (sometimes accelerated by the growing assertiveness of workers, in Japan as well as in France or Italy), but also the cost of fixed capital (buildings and machines) in relation to total workforce began to rise. A relatively simple economic calculation shows that in these conditions, allowing for inflation, firms' profitability (relationship between annual profit and fixed capital) is bound to fall.

The basic cause of these unfortunate developments is to be found at the centre of the Fordist labour process model: the crisis of the worker's 'paradoxical involvement' where Taylorism dominates. The weaknesses of these organizational principles were revealed, in the context of relative full employment at the end of the 1960s, by a worldwide wave of revolts or 'micro-conflicts' in firms and offices, by workers stripped of their initiative and dignity by Taylorism. So long as young people, women and those straight from the countryside or the Third World were entering the labour force, 'discipline' was maintained; nevertheless, as time passed, better education, greater self-awareness among groups of workers, and a widespread desire for work satisfaction and dignity led to an increasingly open revolt against the denial of personality by the starkest forms of separation between those who designed and those who performed tasks.

Ten years later, the revolts had become a general left-wing upsurge, and employers' attempts to 'make workers pay for the crisis' had been met by strikes, often successful ones. However, towards the end of the 1970s, in France, Italy, Britain – in fact, everywhere in Europe as well as in North America – this surge had come to an end. The 'privileged' – those who had kept their jobs – were surrounded by a growing tide of unemployment. The threat of redundancy re-established discipline in factories. However, the crisis was still there. Productivity gains had virtually disappeared; investment was more costly with each year; profit margins remained depressed.

The reason went deeper than the fact that Taylorist principles had led to revolt: the principles themselves, by separating 'the scientific organization of work' from its unskilled performance, had in the end dried up the source of productivity gains. Since most workers were formally excluded from the fight for productivity and product quality, and since even the idea that they were subjectively involved was rejected, an increasingly small number of engineers and technical staff found themselves with the task of improving collective skills; but they could only raise workers' productivity by means of increasingly complex and costly machines which they designed for them.

The reaction of firms to falling profitability was to put a higher mark-up on the price of their goods, thus increasing cost inflation. This was self-sustaining, since the mechanisms of Fordist regulation meant that price rises led to wage increases, and so on. When price rises outstripped wage increases, purchasing power, and therefore demand, fell; economic activity slowed in certain sectors (construction, or the automobile industry) and brought the risk of a generalized recession, which Fordist regulation had managed until then to avert.

Inevitably, the whole miraculous balance of the Fordist compromise was jeopardized. Not only did the rate of investment fall with the drop in real profit margins, but each new investment led to fewer jobs, as labour was replaced by fixed capital. The slowdown in real wage increases to offset the drop in real profit margins depressed markets, and increased unemployment. But Fordist logic implied more unemployment benefit, and more social welfare; which is what happened in the first half of the 1970s. This 'safety net' prevented the collapse of domestic demand in major capitalist countries, unlike the crisis of the 1930s. However, these social transfers eventually had to be paid for by taxes or contributions; this placed too great a burden on the active part of the economy (wages as well as profits), which led to a further drop in the profitability of investment. In the end, the very legitimacy of the welfare state and welfare benefits was called into question, and with it, the whole Fordist compromise.

In this way, for purely internal reasons, the Fordist compromise (subordination of workers to managerial staff and machines, in exchange for the promise of a steady job and steadily increasing consumer power) became economically unsustainable for employers in the 1970s, ten years after the revolt of young people and some workers signalled their moral condemnation of a 'unidimensional society' which could offer only the option of 'wasting one's life earning one's living'. However, the reason for the crisis was not a 'saturation of demand': as long as purchasing power is available, demand remains limitless. Moreover, many groups in advanced capitalist countries, as well as inhabitants of the Third World, were not part of the 'consumer society'; and the burning desire to consume remained strong among the rich – they simply reduced their rate of saving from the early 1970s onwards.

Instead, the crisis of the Fordist development model should be seen primarily as a supply-side crisis – a crisis of the labour process, which, because it dehumanizes the worker, ends up by not being efficient, even from the employer's point of view.

To keep my argument clear, I have not yet mentioned another important aspect of the crisis of the Fordist development model – the ecological crisis. When it first appeared its full impact was not obvious, but since it affects both the Fordist and the liberal-productivist model, it will be discussed later, in Chapter 5.

The internationalization of the crisis

Another chain of events, a totally perverse one, also contributed to the breakdown of the virtuous circle of Fordist growth – internationalization. From the end of the 1960s, the competitiveness of Japan and Europe (at the prevailing dollar exchange rate) had reached and overtaken that of the United States. The American trade balance became structurally in deficit. As its first fighting devaluation, and the first shot in the trade war, the dollar abandoned its ties with gold, which were in any case only theoretical.

The trade war intensified when the 1973 oil shock enabled oil producers to take their 'cut' from Fordist revenues. In the immediate term, profitability fell even further, but the most obvious effect was to force countries to export more to pay (on credit, that is) for their energy imports. However, even without the oil factor, increased internationalization was inevitable in the struggle to stop Fordism disintegrating.

To recover their profitability, multinational companies spread their operations over entire continents, and forged subcontracting links with certain Third World countries which, ten years later, were to become the 'newly industrialized countries'. World trade began to grow much more quickly than demand in individual countries. The management of growth became less and less amenable to government control.

Whereas previously any increase in real wages in a Fordist country resulted mainly in increased demand for domestic products, internationalization meant that foreign suppliers entered the fray: increased purchasing power meant more consumption and investment, and therefore more imports. The obvious response was to export more, but this meant selling more cheaply abroad. The only solution was to keep wage increases below gains in productivity. For imports as well as exports, to achieve the right trade balance, each country was obliged to damp down its domestic demand, and look to others to absorb its surplus production. Unfortunately, trading partners were doing exactly the same, leading to the kind of demand-side crisis which post-war Fordist regulation had eliminated in the national context.

There was, of course, no multinational agreement to balance growth in different countries, no international collective agreements, no supranational welfare state, no international treaty on working hours. To the supply-side internal crisis of Fordism was added a demand-side international crisis.

Fordism was caught between a fall in profits (because of the unsolved crisis of the labour process) and a drop in demand (because there was no effective international mode of regulation); its lingering death was characterized by alternating attempts to prop up demand, which foundered on a supply-side crisis, and efforts to restore profit margins, which came to grief because of weak demand.

The first three stages

The emphasis during the first period, from 1973 to 1979, was on 'stimulating domestic demand'. The US Federal Reserve's benign neglect in issuing dollars, and the consequent flooding of the Eurodollar market, meant that any internal adjustment was postponed and OPEC surpluses could be absorbed and recycled to newly industrialized countries. This management of world demand was, in its way, cooperative; but it did not produce miracles, since crisis in the supply side was ignored. Profits continued to fall, conflicts about sharing growth were mitigated by rising inflation, and the dollar fell in value.

The first turning point was in 1979, when 'experts' and governments came round to the opposite solution: restrict credit to eliminate 'lame ducks', favour firms with a bright future, and dilute social welfare provision to boost profits and therefore, it was claimed, investment. This reorganization of the operating environment was to give free rein to the invisible hand of the market and provide a rapid solution to the crisis. This 'monetarist' second stage, led by the US Federal Reserve, heralded the era of liberal-productivism, which is examined in Chapter 4.

Competition in the market for goods and services, and in the money markets, meant that this policy came to dominate the rest of the world, even the left-wing government in France. Demand plummeted and interest rates became prohibitive; governments had to damp down their economies to reduce their deficits. However, this monetarist phase came to a sudden stop, just short of catastrophe, in summer 1982, after three years of recession and bankruptcies.

The third stage took a kind of middle way, in that the Federal Reserve partially relaxed credit restraint, the budget deficit boosted domestic demand, and the United States began a long period of expansion, provoking economic activity in the rest of the world. However, there were significant differences from the 'Carter years' of the first stage.

Firstly, the 1960s had thrown up two schools of thought on how to cope with the 'supply-side crisis'. One (mainly in the United States, Britain and France) strongly advocated reducing the cost of labour, by more casual work, sub-contracting and locating production in the Third World. The other, to be found in Japan, Scandinavia and some parts of West Germany and Italy, stressed the need for a new social compromise. This meant encouraging workers to go for quality and productivity, and forging partnership links between firms, higher education and local government.

The success of the second approach became obvious in the mid-1980s, when the Reagan administration's two successive policies proved incapable of stemming the fall in US competitiveness, and particularly in productivity. A combination of this fall, an expansionist budget and an overvalued dollar led to a massive increase in the US trade deficit. This time (the second difference from the Carter years) the deficit was made up not by printing dollars but by US Treasury loans from West Germany and Japan, which were in surplus. The result was that the dollar and interest rates rose.

The third difference was that economic recovery from higher military spending and lower taxes was not evenly spread throughout society: millions of jobs were created (the unemployment rate fell to 5.6 per cent in 1987), but they were low-pay jobs which depended on the trickle-down effect of middle-class spending. A huge 'domestic army' of parking-lot attendants, supermarket-trolley pushers and fast-food workers made the United States into the 'Brazil of the 1980s', a credit-based miracle where a third of the labour force had no social welfare protection.

The fate of the newly industrialized countries was mixed. Those which used their external debt to build up export industries while consolidating self-sufficiency in food and manufactured goods (such as South Korea and Taiwan) gained enormously from US growth and were in a position to service their debts. On the other hand, those borrowing for domestic projects of low profitability or dubious social value had no room for manoeuvre, even with a surplus trade balance with industrialized countries – Brazil's surplus was between 10 and 14 billion dollars a year.

A simplified world picture at the end of the third stage (the end of the 1980s) would be as follows: the US government orders sophisticated armaments from West coast firms, which buy German machine tools; their engineers buy Japanese cars and microcomputers made in South Korea, and pay their 'collective servants' a pittance to buy Brazilian shoes. California imports twice as much as it exports. The Federal government, whose tax revenue is less than its spending, borrows the dollars it needs by selling Treasury bills to Japanese and German exporters.

By 1987, the United States had a trade deficit of $160 billion, while Japan had a surplus of $96 billion ($56 billion with the United States), West Germany $65 billion, OPEC $26 billion and non-OPEC developing countries $36 billion. However, for the last of these, the current account balance was negative (by $12 billion) if one discounts the 'four little dragons' of Asia, whose current account surplus was $38 billion.

Interest rates had to be raised by US banks, to offset Third World non-payment of debt, and by the Federal Reserve, to attract saving from countries in surplus. This increase restrained growth throughout the world. It only needed an argument about this increase between West Germany and the United States in autumn 1987 to cause investors, realizing these imbalances, to sell off their shares and provoke the stock exchange crash.

The world held its breath; but although the 'great economists' issued a 'solemn warning' (Plantu's cartoon in *Le Monde* ironized 'That'll do a lot of good'!), nothing came of it. The central banks printed extra banknotes which brought interest rates down and allowed the stock exchanges to recover. After two months' hesitation, the US government promised to produce a plan to bring down the budget deficit, then did nothing about it; and in the election year 1987–8, the deficit increased further. With a weak dollar, low interest rates and taxes, massive government buying and employment legislation which allowed servants to be paid a pittance for any lousy job, the American economy went full steam ahead, and the unemployment figures continued to show a fall. The trade deficit, of course, continued to rise at the staggering rate of $11 billion a month. By the end of 1988, US external borrowing was over $500 billion, nearly half that of the whole Third World. Nevertheless, George Bush won the 1988 election by a small but decisive margin; and the world continued to follow its crazy course.

Most economists and all ecologists are now convinced that things cannot go on like that. The world economy is like one of those cartoon characters who walk over the edge of a cliff but do not fall because they have not noticed their predicament; which means that when they do fall, it is more catastrophic . . .

3
What Should Be Done?

The question of solutions to the crisis is fundamentally a political one, as it was in the 1930s. However, it is no longer a matter of selecting the right economic policy in line with existing ground rules, but of establishing new rules – new principles for the labour process, new norms on the direction and social use of production, new habits and new modes of regulation. We must agree on new promises and new projects; we must invent a new 'grand compromise'.

It must not be thought that the 'right' solution is dictated by economic laws which are immutable; we need new laws. Nor must it be thought that the crisis is an inevitable calamity, or a difficult stage in the process of change. At the very heat of the crisis is a choice about our future world – witness the success stories of countries such as Japan, South Korea and Sweden where, in the last twenty years, there has been both growth and full employment, a higher standard of living and, sometimes, enhanced democracy, and where this success has not been jeopardized by a high level of borrowing. The strategies of these countries were, and remain, different: they cannot easily be transferred to other countries, and neither can their long-term stability be assessed. They are proof, however, that there is no 'fate' condemning a country, because of some feature or other that it has, to a permanent back seat – not its size, nor its location in the Third World . . . or in Europe.

We are not stuck in the middle of the stream; we are at

the crossroads. The point has just been made, and will be repeated later, that as yet no overreaching solution has been found, that there is no agreed answer. In other words, no solution stands out as *the* model, just as there is no unchanging world order. The 'third stage' of the crisis led to the October 1987 stock market crash, and a distinctive fourth stage was only just beginning to emerge at the end of the 1980s. The monetarist and neo-liberal principles of the early 1980s have lost their prestige, but they are by no means politically discredited.

If the impasse is a political one, does this mean that economists have nothing to contribute? If the way out of the crisis is open-ended, if the future is merely a matter of choosing alternatives, does this mean that everything is possible? Of course not. The problems are clear cut, so in theory the solutions are circumscribed. And in fact, only a limited number of ways forward have been explored since the early 1970s.

In these circumstances, the part which economists can play is significant, provided they can break free from abstract models or dogmatic justification of existing situations. Above all, economists can explain the difficulties which wrecked the 'old compromises' and which shut the door on a 'return to the golden age'. They can point to the difficulties, even the contradictions and lack of logic, which will wreck the grand designs of particular political groups. But only political groups as the expression of profound social movements will be responsible for what will finally emerge, for future grand compromises, for new development models. For this reason, when economists propose solutions which they have worked out, they claim to be *concerned citizens*, or even political activists. In other words, within the range of possible action which economists have identified (assuming they have done a good job of work as economists, free from the blinkers of ideological preferences, however high-minded these might be), they choose, in the name of moral criteria and a world view which is part of the spirit of the times, a specific response to the objective problems of the period. Knowledge of economic reality will simply have helped towards a better awareness of the 'real' problems.

What are these? If my analysis up to now is correct, they can be grouped under two headings:

• problems stemming from those weaknesses in the previous development model which became apparent on a 'country-by-country basis', relating to the crisis of work, the consumption model, the crisis of the welfare state and also the ecological crisis;
• problems arising from the contradiction between the increasingly internationalized nature of production and markets and the resolutely national character of the 'modes of regulation' which, in the golden age of Fordism, gave clear-cut solutions relevant to that era.

What is immediately striking is the *political asymmetry* of these problems. It seems that those in the first group can be solved at the national level, and perhaps even the local level (apart, as we shall see later, from certain ecological problems which are global in nature). In other words there is at the outset a framework, where political choice is to some degree effective, for conflicts and for the compromises to resolve them. Even civil war is resolved in a national framework. Democracy is a system which more or less works ('the worst system apart from all the others'), but we can make it work only in the national context. Here, in theory, the sovereign people chooses at election time between several models on offer, and it is the responsibility of directly accountable public authorities to implement the choice. Any problems in this representative, 'formal' democracy can, it seems, be solved by further reducing their geographical scope, in that it is often thought (not without reason) that compromises which cannot be reached at national level can be found at regional or local level.

The snag is, however, that debates at the local or national level are no use if the compromises reached are merely straws in the fierce wind of the world market, for which no sovereignty is a match – certainly not, at the present time, democratic sovereignty. If there are modes of regulation to resolve the contradictions of the international economy, they can be established only in one of two ways:

• through the influence of one or more dominant countries. This hegemony would need to be 'armoured in coercion' (to use Gramsci's hallowed phrase), so that the world's leading power also acts as the world's police. This is what happened, as we have seen, in the case of US hegemony, under which Fordism on a national basis flourished;
• through the unanimous, and therefore negotiated, agreement of most countries.

The second method, which of course is the one I prefer, involves a major problem. Unlike the first approach, where the 'leader' dictates not only national models but also the world order to go with them, the unanimous agreement method brings together countries which have no *a priori* reason on the basis of their own social conflicts, domestic pacts or electoral decisions to choose or desire the same development model. It is their full right and privilege to opt for different ones.

Let us assume that economists have come up with two models as a way out of the crisis – the 'grasshopper model' of minimal work and frugal living, and the 'ant model', implying hard work to improve one's lot.[1] These 'models' are no doubt incompatible where goods are traded freely. The world economic order which can be agreed on is not necessarily the most appropriate for either model. We need a model allowing some to be 'ants' and others to be 'grasshoppers'. Even economists fully committed to either model can suggest no political means to make not only their own fellow citizens, but also the citizens of other countries, adopt the development model whose virtues they are extolling. Of course, they may well take sides where, in another country, there is a bitter conflict between two opposing visions of society; they may well go to fight and die in Madrid, but the Spanish war is fought in Spain.

In these circumstances, the only possible kind of international agreement is one which maximizes the range of choice for the different 'democratic collectivities'. This term is deliberately used instead of 'nation' because there are intermediate situations where democratic choice and social compromise are located 'above' the national level – I am thinking of course of Europe, to which we will return later.

There are, however, areas where global sovereignty is necessary, where the simple realization of our 'common humanity' ought to make us recognize a 'world law' superior to national freedom of choice. One thinks immediately of apartheid in South Africa; and, in the choice of development model, ecological problems must obviously be borne in mind.

A country's citizens obviously have the right to choose, by majority decision, to live in a cloud of exhaust fumes and eat hormone-fed veal, provided the country in question does not insist on exporting its veal. International trade agreements can allow countries to set their own health standards, as a derogation from absolute free trade. The problem arises when exhaust fumes and other effluents begin to cross frontiers, destroy the ozone layer, create global warming, spread radioactive particles. Freedom to choose a development model stops where it impinges on that of other countries; it can no longer prevail when the future of the planet is at stake.

That which seemed the best solution in the 1980s, but whose fate seemed to be in the balance as the third stage of the crisis neared its end, was neither 'ant' nor 'grasshopper'. At national and international level, it was, and still is, the model of the free-running fox in the free-range chicken pen.[2] It was well and truly on its way to becoming the only solution. In succession, not only the United States and Britain, but also Mitterrand's France and the social democrats of Southern Europe, adopted it in one form or other. So did Jaruzelski's Poland and Deng Xiaoping's China. However, the final outcome is still undecided, as we shall see on closer analysis.

4

The Impasses of Liberal-Productivism

Liberal-productivism can be defined as the world view (or 'societal paradigm') which inspired the major turning point of the end of the 1970s, bringing to power Margaret Thatcher in Britain and Ronald Reagan in the United States. It came to dominate most international economic advisory and regulatory bodies (OECD, IMF, the World Bank), was adopted by European socialists, and was behind the emergence (at least in outline) of a completely new development model in the 1980s. The model, as has already been said, is no longer very plausible, though it had a profound effect on the world order as well as on the reality facing a large number of countries. In France, liberal-productivism dominates the broad centre ground stretching from the RPR[1] to the Socialist Party, since a paradigm always has a right and a left. This world view was founded on the ruins of Fordism in crisis, from whose downfall comes its major strength.

A new model

What liberal-productivism propounds is more or less as follows: we are experiencing a 'technological revolution'; however, in the 1970s, constraints imposed by the state and trade unions – social provision, welfare state, anti-pollution laws and the like – stopped it developing freely, by starving firms of capital, and by preventing 'painful but necessary changes'. Therefore, the argument went, let us get rid of the constraints; stop subsidizing lame ducks and bureaucratic and inefficient public services, and raise interest rates to deter non-profitable activity. In this way, the free market would automatically establish a new development model in line with new technologies. These are essentially flexible because of the scope of their application, and therefore able to respond to varied and individualized demand, which the state cannot regulate. New technologies also need, because of the huge investment involved, direct deployment on a global scale, not amenable to control by even the largest states.

This kind of argument reflects the optimism of the triumphant nineteenth-century bourgeoisie – an unshakeable confidence in the virtues of the 'development of productive forces', which could only be harmed by the constraints of outmoded legal rules and practices. This optimism embraced both the old liberals and the first Marxists, the only difference being that the former thought there was 'too much state control' and the latter that there was 'too much anarchy in the market'.

It is important to stress, however, a major difference between nineteenth-century liberalism and contemporary liberal-productivism. The former tried to ensure the happiness of all by encouraging the citizen to seek individual enrichment. It was a 'utilitarian', 'hedonistic' liberalism, where the goal of technical progress and free enterprise was happiness through the enrichment of all.

Of course, the best exponents of the new liberalism, such as Ronald Reagan, do not ignore this aspect. However, very often and particularly in France, its language has been stripped of its appeal, reduced to the cold necessity of the nature of things. Deregulation, free trade, technological change have come to dominate, like three mice chasing their tails, running round in a circle whose illogicality simply shows how impossible it is to stop. To the question 'Why do we really need free trade and free enterprise?', the answer is 'To modernize the productive system', and to the question 'Why modernize the productive system?', the reply is 'To cope with international competition'. In other words, an unequivocal return to what in the past was unspoken: 'Accumulate, accumulate, that is the Law and the prophets.' 'Productive modernization' becomes a categorical imperative, as philosophers would say, and free trade, free enterprise, flexibility and deregulation are its tools. There is no longer a need for higher justification of a political or moral nature.

This does not mean that liberal-productivism need no longer concern itself with justifications, or with creating a social consensus. Building this cohesion, however, is no longer the priority of economic policy, and it is doubtful whether it is still an objective of policy as such. The 'homeland', the collectivity to which the citizen has allegiance, becomes the firm or the market.

Within the firm, managers and workers constitute a community: everybody is in the same boat, as it were. They stand shoulder to shoulder – or tighten their belts – to weather the storm of competition. The task of trade unions – if there are any left – is no longer to protect workers' interests against employers' interests. The authority of the heads of businesses has to be respected; the most that can be done is to give them firm advice on improving collective efficiency in the interests of everybody – that is, of the members of the business threatened by the outside world.

The market gives everyone with enterprise and fighting spirit the chance to 'win'; not to 'win something', but simply to win, to beat other people. The Socialist Party slogan in the 1986 elections was '*Vive la France qui gagne.*' Of course, there have to be losers as well, but this is the cost of having the winners giving consumers the best services, the best products (here the tone of liberal-productivism becomes 'progressist' again). Moreover, if you go to the wall, the success of others gives you a second chance; if you do not ask for too much, you can live on crumbs from rich people's tables, by being their servants, shining their shoes, showing them to their seats in high-class restaurants . . .

Who looks after the others – the ill, the handicapped, the permanently unemployed and unemployable? Not the state, or at least to the minimum degree, just enough to avoid 'unrest'; let their relatives and neighbours look after them. Pierre Rosanvallon[2] called this 'reintegrating solidarity into civil society'. To hell with the bureaucratic ways of the welfare state; to hell with the administrative approach to solidarity! 'Civil society' (that is, everything which is not the state) will take over. It amounts to a return to the oldest 'welfare' – the voluntary sector – and to its 'natural specialists' (women), who in their work and domestic duties bandage the wounds of victims of the all-in struggle.

A rough attempt to define the 'societal paradigm' of liberal-productivism would be as follows:

- greater emphasis on the productivist techno-economic imperative, now 'categorical', and the disappearance of the very idea of an explicit choice of society deriving from democracy (invest because of the need to export, export because of the need to invest);
- fragmentation of social existence, with firms playing the role previously performed by the mother country (we must stand together against competitors), and the world market becoming the operating environment;
- a wide variety of ways to integrate the individual into the firm, from straightforward discipline to negotiated involvement, but all on the basis of the individual, not of collective individuality (class or job solidarity);
- an overall reduction of administrative-type solidarity

based on belonging to a national collectivity, with 'civil society' (meaning quite simply the family) supposed to take over responsibility for what the welfare state can no longer guarantee.

In the final analysis, it amounts to a hierarchical individualism, where firstly individuals' adherence to the collectivity is justified only if it is in their interest, and the collectivity does not concern itself with the interest of its individuals; and where secondly the collectivity acquires collective meaning only through the individualism of those who dominate it – that is, the 'winners' – in whose interest it might be to take losers under their wing.

Any criticism of the impasses in this model must be preceded by an assessment of its rationality and effectiveness. It is a model which certainly stands up to analysis, and which can carry the day. By 1985, it appeared to be doing so, just as corporatism and its Fascist variants seemed destined to carry all before them around 1938. The liberal-productivist model offers a kind of stability which is questionable but real. In the past, feudal lords 'offered' their peasants protection against attack by other lords, and also land in return for work. A particular social order was justified by the existence of generalized conflict, and the overall system remained stable for a long time. Naturally it was continually disturbed by wars and incursions and gratuitous revolts, but it was precisely this fact which made a feudal hierarchy acceptable as protection against the harsh conditions of the period.

Can liberal-productivism, however, be satisfied with this kind of overall stability based on permanent instability at the micro-level? It is precisely this which became open to doubt in the second half of the 1980s. The tensions in the model will now be analysed.

A society torn apart

Above all, liberal-productivism leads to intense social polarization. The result can be described as a 'two-tier society' or an 'hourglass society', with people above and people below, and the centre getting squeezed. This is what is happening with the spectacular 'Latin-Americanization' (or 'Brazilianization') of the United States. On top, the winners in the competition (the rich, the powerful, the decision makers, the bruisers) will benefit from the advantages of the technological revolution, in so far as there are any. In the middle, an increasingly smaller and more destabilized group of semi-skilled workers will no doubt benefit from a certain level of welfare protection, particularly in the employment field, but they cannot expect increases in real wages, as they could under Fordism. At the bottom, a mass of 'job seekers' will be buffetted between casual work and unemployment. When unemployed, their lot will be more or less improved by public charity or help from their families, depending on how far local government authorities adopt a humanized version of the liberal model. As with feudalism, the fate of the poor depends on the 'Christian spirit' of others.

The political implications of developments like this are obvious: we are back again to the famous nineteenth-century 'problem of the dangerous classes', with the possibility of mass revolts destabilizing the system (the best possible result in my opinion), or the spread of individual crime. The latter case would be a return to the regulation principle of liberalism, when fear united the top two thirds of society, and even some of the lower third, against the 'threat' of crime. The 'law and order' issue as a political argument is all the more effective in that troublemakers can be isolated as 'outsiders', as can those neatly summed up as 'predelinquents'[3] – black people, young people from rundown housing complexes, and the like. One might even start a lucrative line of business by hiring some poor people as security guards to defend the rich against other poor people.

From Rio de Janeiro to Los Angeles, the model has shown it can work. It seems to have a great future: any collective action by the 'lower third' which would, as before, allow the vicious circle to be broken by moving from individual action to the 'class struggle', is now severely constrained by the collapse of collective secular ideals following on the collapse of Fordism. Collective idealism very often takes refuge in archaic forms such as religious sects, fundamentalism, and the like. It is only through a progressive world view, different from Fordist-type progressive thinking (Marxist in Europe, developmentalist-nationalist in the Third World), that a struggle to free the oppressed and the marginalized can be started again. There is still a long way to go, but the fate of liberal-productivism depends on taking this major step, which could be a great risk or a major opportunity.

A false way out of Taylorism

Already, however, the model encounters another problem, concerned with production. Given the mode of regulation of the wage relation which usually prevails in neo-liberal thinking, there is quite simply no solution to the crisis of the Fordist labour-process model. In fact, by reducing as far as possible institutional links between the firm and its workers, and by encouraging casual work, there is a danger of an even greater gap between workers and the jobs they do – workers are even less consciously involved in the fight for productivity and quality.

Of course, it is in the famous 'technological revolution'

that the answer to this problem is sought. In car body shops or on printed circuit production lines, robots, by performing flawlessly 24 hours a day and never going on strike, will solve the problem of workers slowing the pace of assembly lines or being no good at their work.

Unfortunately 'technology', even electronic, is not something which works on its own. It represents certain forms of cooperation between work already done to create machines, and the living work (on the line or not) of operatives, technicians and engineers. In theory, automated technology allows us to get rid of any conscious involvement, even informal and paradoxical, by line workers – it merely needs engineers to design the necessary machines and technicians to install and adjust them properly; then you simply let illiterate people feed the Beast with raw material and reams of computerized data, and sweep up the debris afterwards! These unskilled people are easily replaced from the armies of unemployed waiting to take over. Relations such as these between the conception and execution of work are even easier to establish between large firms and subcontractors, on an inter-regional or international level. Large firms set up in urban areas with highly qualified, highly paid staff, monopolize the design of machines and the sale of end products, and subcontract the actual manufacture to satellite firms operating in poorer areas with widespread unemployment.

A labour process model of this kind, which can be called 'neo-Taylorist', is of course quite conceivable, and is the norm in the United States, Britain and France, in the service sector as well as manufacturing. Taken to the extreme, workshops would be like space exploration modules sent to Jupiter by engineers sitting behind their desks on Earth. Fine, but what if something goes wrong? In a space probe, each part has a back-up and a double back-up; in an automated workshop, you have to call out the after-sales or maintenance service of the firm supplying the machine, which brings us back to the main problem with Taylorism – there is a race to automate (and therefore to invest), and there are lower 'on-the-spot' productivity gains because there are no people actually working on, adjusting and improving the machines on a permanent basis.

Why has the technology of automation been applied in this way rather than others? Basically for political reasons – the politics of production line and office. Whereas the original aim of Taylorism was to end the explicit and essential involvment of craftworkers' skills, neo-Taylorism tries to eliminate the residual, hidden and paradoxical involvement of the unskilled worker, of the supermarket cashier, of the office typist. It was natural that in the 1970s, neo-Taylorism triumphed in situations where operatives rejected this paradoxical involvement and showed this in absenteeism, work-to-rules, slowing the assembly line. In its Turin factory, the Fiat management set up the almost totally automated workshops of Robotgate, Digitron and LAM in order to have no workers present in the most troublesome sectors. The aim was to re-establish managerial authority; the cost of automation far exceeded the investment needed for optimal technical efficiency. At the beginning of the 1980s, after Fiat's 'Fordist' workers had been defeated, the management had to admit that 'the LAM system, designed at a time when industrial relations had broken down, is an interesting but one-off development. It is very expensive, takes up a huge amount of space and breaks down more frequently than a less sophisticated installation.'[4]

The alternative, which I and many employers, including Italian ones, advocate, is obviously to go for systems which are 'less sophisticated' but which mobilize the skills of line workers, in real time, at the actual point of production. Out goes 'paradoxical' involvement; in comes dialogue between machine design, machine maintenance and line production; even, perhaps, amalgamation of the second and third functions. This would mean groups of workers, highly skilled in more than one area, being able to adjust and repair their machines, and to advise and even co-operate with the designers. This would have to go hand in hand with improved relations between firms involved in the same production process – continuous interaction and dialogue between those which design machines and those which use them. Subcontracting would be replaced by 'partnership'.

The 1980s showed that in countries where firms opted for this labour-process model, such as Japan, West Germany, Sweden and, in the end, northern Italy, the introduction of new technology was much more efficient; this is shown by the fact that this group of countries gained from the trade war. In other words, there are signs in the present day and age that we can turn on its head the age-old tendency of capitalism, pushed to its culmination by Taylorism, to separate the manual aspects of work from the intellectual ones.

However, what would be the cost of reuniting what Taylor separated? If employers recognize their employees' skill and initiative, how would they turn these to their own benefit, and what would they be prepared to pay for their employees' greater commitment to work? The immediate answer of many employers (particularly in France) trying to introduce the illusory Japanese concept of 'quality circles' would be . . . nothing. 'We are giving you greater job satisfaction. It is you who should thank us.' Sometimes it works, for a time – with men, for example, who find it amusing for a short time. But women physically resent the fact that, while the new system might engage their attention and their intelligence, they have no time to think about their 'second job' – shopping, planning meals, childcare. For the same wage, they would prefer flow-process work to working in 'modules'. Management is simply confirmed in its contempt for 'manual workers'.

What is worse is that 'liberal' modes of regulation of the wage relation, by putting more emphasis on 'flexibility' and casual work, mean it is virtually impossible for employees to feel consciously involved in improving the labour process or ensuring quality products or services in 'their' firm. To be 'involved', employees must feel that their long-term interest is tied to that of their firm. The only solution is for them to get something in return; in other words, we need a new 'grand compromise'.

One possible approach to this is through individual negotiation, where, in return for involvement, workers receive bonuses, promotion or merit increases in pay; if they do not want to be involved, they can leave. This leads to bargaining in skills and involvement, inside and outside the firm – a kind of 'institutionalized boot-licking'. Workers sell to their employer not only their time, but also their readiness to cooperate more than their colleagues. This model, based on competition between skilled employees, has been called 'Californian' by Philippe Messine,[5] a term based on the market in computer staff in the famous Silicon Valley. Unlike the 'wage society' of the Fordist model, where even managing directors thought of themselves as employees, different from semi-skilled workers only in being further up the scale, what is happening is a 'rebargaining' of the wage relation: employees are all individual entrepreneurs, but some sell their labour directly to others for a fee.

This model, quite different from neo-Taylorism as far as the labour process is concerned, is in fact perfectly compatible with it in the context of liberal-productivism, but it does not apply to the same segment of the labour force. It is quite possible to have, in the same factory or the same office, neo-Taylorism for the unskilled and semi-skilled, and an 'individually negotiated involvement' for more qualified employees.

We can take this line of reasoning further: there can be

guaranteed employment and collective bargaining in major firms, while neo-Taylorism is kept for women, immigrants and handicapped people in subcontracting firms and consumer services such as fast food. Japan, or the Germany described in Günter Wallraff's book *Lowest of the Low*,[6] are examples of this two-tier society, in which the upper echelons of the labour force retain Fordist social benefits from the past and are intimately involved in the fight for quality and productivity, while the rest are condemned to neo-Taylorist casual employment.

In this type of labour-process model, which Masahiko Aoki, a Japanese expert in labour economics, calls 'workers' democracy',[7] we are outside the scope of liberal-productivist principles *as far as the firm is concerned*. The 'freedom of entrepreneurs' is in fact strictly limited by the contract which ties them to their employees, either implicitly by custom or explicitly by collective agreement. In exchange for employees' commitment, their jobs are guaranteed and they are continually involved in negotiations about technical changes and similar matters.

To call this 'workers' democracy' is probably going too far, but Aoki stresses the 'dilemma of workers' democracy': firms where the practice is to negotiate involvement collectively have to be careful, because they operate in a liberal world. Their employees can be guaranteed something in return only to the extent that their commitment leads to higher sales, and this is not certain, since the market may collapse or a rival firm may out-perform them. Because of this, the collective compromise has to be limited to the smallest possible stable group of employees – a kind of wage-earners' *aristocracy*, fighting off 'dangerous competitors'; that is, other employees. This is another example of the feudal model, except that some of the villeins have beome knights in league with the lord against the rest.

The compromise which I will propose will be much more

advantageous for all employees; but it remains true that the Japanese compromise is far more attractive, even from the capitalist point of view, than Anglo-Saxon or French liberal-productivism . . .

The return of economic instability

The third major problem with liberal-productivism is macroeconomic – the recurrence of crises of over-production, and periodic 1930-style slumps in the social demand, as happened in Britain and the United States in the early 1980s and as will happen again (as in 1989–90) when they bring down their trade deficit to manageable proportions.

In the case of Fordism, growth in demand is in a sense programmed. Entrepreneurs are guaranteed expanding markets, since all employers give their employees wage rises more or less in unison. It is therefore in their interest to invest, which in itself calls for more capital goods, spreads wages around, and so on. With regulation under liberalism, entrepreneurs get hints on market trends only by observing the behaviour of other entrepreneurs. They invest if they think their neighbours' 'investment mood' is on the upswing (economists call this 'animal spirits'). The behaviour of each entrepreneur therefore validates the guesses of the others, until a few bankers, wholesalers or entrepreneurs see that demand does not match recent investment, and the result is panic, stock market crashes and drop in output.

The classic solution to this lack of demand management, when there is no explicitly coordinated increase in total wages, is public spending on major investment projects or armaments. What a paradox! A liberal-productivist regime of accumulation only works well with a high-spending government which keeps taxes low! This is what happened in the United States from 1983 to 1988. By 1987 everybody had come to think that growth based on such a deficit could not go on, which led to the stock market crash. However, since the deficit remained high, US growth continued in 1988; and other countries, seeing the United States simply carrying on, carried on as well. As we shall see, this situation cannot last for ever, because of the balance of international payments – a country cannot continue to drag others along by piling up debts.

The great international disorder

The fourth problem facing liberal-productivism in its international dimension is free trade. As we have seen, the golden age of Fordism did not go down the road of an untrammeled open-market system which was the favoured grand design of the United States after World War II. In their long-term interest, they allowed the reconstruction of Japan and Western Europe to take place within a certain degree of protectionism. At the same time, independent Third World countries applied protectionism in their development policy, but they were not serious rivals. Things began to go wrong in the late 1960s, when first Western Europe and Japan and then the newly industrialized countries reached North American levels of competitiveness either by achieving comparable productivity or by having much lower wage levels. Markets and even production channels became internationalized, but at the international level there was still no regulatory mechanism to manage growth in demand that was comparable to Fordist compromises at national level.

The response of liberal-productivism to these problems was somewhat illogical – it called for even less organization, even fewer regulatory mechanisms. Free trade was supposed to work automatically to bring about both the 'adjustment' of economies to each other, and the mutual encouragement of growth. Not only did neither happen, but what was worse, the only way in which free trade can 'adjust' international imbalances (those which reduce deficits in countries with too many imports and too few exports, or allow them to attract capital investment and loans) has the effect of restricting growth world-wide. In fact, growth in the 1970s and 1980s was gained at the expense of greater imbalances.

It is useful to remind ourselves that imbalances were worse as a result of the oil shocks: non-oil-exporting countries had to increase exports of other commodities to pay for imported oil. As long as they paid 'on credit' – that is, without reducing their deficit – things went reasonably well (the 'first stage of the crisis'). Then the United States cut its deficit by reducing domestic demand (second stage), thereby dragging the rest of the world into recession. Then it went for growth again, pulling the rest with it, but . . . by increasing its deficit.

Basically, it is very logical. In a free-trade situation, trade deficits arise when certain countries expand too quickly for their capacity to produce competitively. And, as we have seen, the wrong choice of labour-process model ruined US competitiveness with Japan or West Germany. There are two possible responses to this situation. Either engineer a recession in the country in deficit; or allow it to borrow – that is, *not* to adjust. But if all countries in deficit go into recession by raising taxes or cutting government spending, who will take exports? Alternatively, if countries in deficit borrow, they need to raise interest rates to attract loans; and these high rates soon become the international norm. Entrepreneurs then find financial investments more profitable than producing goods, and stop investing in production.

In all these circumstances, if countries without the common means of regulating growth in demand are put together in a free-trade situation, the result is stagnation or at best spasmodic growth. As we shall see later, the European Community is a good example of this; but the Third World situation is even more dramatic because of the burden of debt from the past. Even a high-export country such as Brazil can have such a high debt burden that it must still continue to force its people to tighten their belts, export more and import less. But when the standard of living is already low, when distribution of wealth is very uneven with the poorest groups well below the national average, as in Brazil or India, and when the population is rising rapidly, what in other countries would be called 'austerity' amounts in these cases to misery, hunger and the agony of a whole people.

When, in 1987, Brazil ended the price freeze which had significantly increased the purchasing power of the poorest groups but curtailed its ability to repay foreign borrowing, within just a few weeks whole families were priced out of their rented homes and had to move to the burgeoning shanty towns. Five years, before, recession in North America had jolted Brazil's export drive at a time when its Noreste province was hit by drought. Ground down by foreign debt, the Brazilian dictatorship rejected the idea of a small reduction in the comfortable living standards of the ruling classes to help the inhabitants of the affected areas. A million people died; I saw the dying crawl into the centre of Recife, the provincial capital. That is what is meant by adjustment!

Reaganism, however, which was responsible in the final analysis for these catastrophes, did not remain unaffected by the impasse to which *laissez-faire* led. When the US trade deficit reached enormous proportions in the mid-1980s, the Reagan administration refused, of course, to impose on its electorate the IMF recipe of recession and huge devaluation. After a period when 'everyone for themselves' was the guiding principle, Reaganism discovered the virtues of negotiation, multilateralism and partnership in international relations, and the active responsibility of states in the regulation of demand. By the end of 1985, the United States suggested that Western Europe (in effect West Germany) and Japan should boost their domestic demand to attract American exports. More than that – they begged them and threatened them, and in the end deliberately weakened the dollar, as the most effective way to protect against imports and subsidize exports.

It did not work as well as expected, and the United States had to move to an increasingly explicit protectionism. The main point, however, for the present argument is that the policy of this intensely free-market government amounted to a return to the old 'cooperative' doctrine of the OECD in the early 1970s; Stephen Marris, who had been the OECD's economic advisor at the time, took his cue from Cato in Ancient Rome and continually advocated such a move. To sum up: the responsibility for world growth lies on those countries with a trade surplus. It is up to them to boost home demand to attract others' exports. And it might be added that if they do not do this, it is perfectly legitimate for countries in deficit to have recourse to protectionism.

The American administration's new multilateralism, for which Bush's secretary of state, James Baker, was responsible, was as far removed from the free-market model as protectionism (one of its weapons) is from free trade. An explicit compromise between states is the only alternative to the all-out war which is at the heart of liberal-productivism. As in the case of the labour process, it is this kind of liberalism which is on the defensive, gradually giving way to a new grand design that is still being defined . . .

This is an important point in favour of the alternative compromise which I am proposing. But before coming to that, we need to look at a crisis common to both productivisms – to Fordism and to the liberalism which is trying to supplant it: in other words, the ecological crisis.

5

The Ecological Crisis

As the twenty-first century approaches, a spectre is haunting the world – that of ecological crisis. And the political scene in Europe is haunted by a minor spectre – ecologist parties. In the nineteenth century, however, socialist parties based on the 'scientific critique of political economy' never called themselves 'economist parties'. The reason is that there is a dissymmetry between ecology and the economy, which gives rise to misunderstanding.

'Economy' and 'ecology' are etymologically very close. 'Economy' is the study of the laws (*nomos*) of the household sphere (*oikos*); 'ecology' is the study of the meaning or rationality (*logos*) of the household sphere. When 'political' is added, this means that the sphere in question is the whole of the 'city' (*polis*). Economy deals with regularities in actions to enhance the sphere; ecology poses the question of whether these actions have a meaning, whether they are reasonable, whether they 'stand up'. More precisely, economy, or economics, is the science of the human activities of production and distribution. Ecology as a science extends this viewpoint: above and beyond the activity itself, it considers the environment where the activity takes place, the interaction between them, and changes in the environment as a result of the activity. The environment is the condition of our existence and of all our activities, under the influence of which, voluntarily or involuntarily, it is constantly changing.

Ecologism is a species of humanism

Nineteenth-century socialism and Communism attacked the political economy of the time for failing to recognize that social conditions were a product of the age and therefore contestable: so one political economy was challenged by another. By contrast, the task of political ecology is even more daunting – to remind people of what they have purely and simply forgotten. People are already 'ideologically' ecologist when they remember that human beings and nature are a single whole, that human beings are part of nature, that nature is being irresistibly altered and humanized, sometimes for the better, but for the worse if one ceases to be aware of it.

This frequently gives rise to the distorted picture of political ecology, for which ecology is sometimes responsible: that there is a conflict between nature in its virgin state and human beings who ravage it. According to this picture, ecologists are people who advocate non-intervention in nature, who for example eat raw plants (especially if they do not eat too many). However, it is unusual for ecologists to fight in defence of the virgin forest (even Chico Mendes advocated a particular *way* of exploiting the Amazon region, against other, less ecologically sound ways). The environment defended by political ecology is mostly artificial: hedgerows, cultivated forests, attractive residential areas, built-up areas to be protected from noise and fumes. In other words, political ecology is mainly urban ecology.

Let us be perfectly clear: ecologism is a species of humanism. It in no way denies the leading role of human beings in nature. Ecology echoes the words of the chorus in Sophocles' *Antigone*:

> Wonders are many on earth and the greatest of these
> Is man, who rides the ocean and takes his way

Through the deeps, through wind-swept valleys of perilous
seas
That surge and sway.

He is master of ageless Earth, to his own will bending
The immortal mother of gods by the sweat of his brow,
As year succeeds to year, with toil unending
Of mule and plough.

He is lord of all things living; birds of the air,
Beasts of the field, all creatures of sea and land
He taketh, cunning to capture and ensnare
With sleight of hand;

Hunting the savage beast from the upland rocks,
Taming the mountain monarch in his lair,
Teaching the wild horse and the roaming ox
His yoke to bear.

The use of language, the wind-swift motion of brain
He learnt; found out the laws of living together
In cities, building him shelter against the rain
And wintry weather.

There is nothing beyond his power. His subtlety
Meeteth all chance, all danger conquereth.
For every ill he hath found its remedy,
Save only death.

O wondrous subtlety of man, that draws
To good or evil ways!

Sophocles: *The Theban Plays* (Penguin
Classics) trans. E. F. Watling

Nothing was left unsaid in this, the earliest period of our
civilization: the power of this 'wonder of the universe', and
the responsibility of human beings. But Sophocles could
not have foreseen the day when the 'grey ocean' was awash
with oil-spills, and the 'ageless Earth' would tire of 'the
sweat of [man's] brow'.

Political ecology was founded on this incontrovertible

fact: the time of the finite earth is beginning. At the start of the twentieth century, when imperialist domination was ending, Paul Valéry wrote of 'the time of the finite world'. Europeans were running out of peoples to rule and colonize. Today, our planet is entirely humanized, no longer a great exterior, a great thermostat. From the ionosphere to the depths of the ocean, from the dry plateaux of the Sahel region to the green lungs of the Amazon, human activity has affected the environment. There is no more unspoilt or widely available nature; no more land or sea not worn out from digesting our waste. We are all responsible in everything we do for the irreparable harm to our environment. What human beings do has always affected nature, sometimes for the better – the eradication of smallpox . . . or AIDS. Improvements in European agriculture, from the seventeenth to the mid-twentieth century, by natural and even, at first, artificial fertilizers, were obviously welcome.

Today, however, crimes against nature are on the increase, and every crime against nature is a crime against humanity. Moreover, they are deliberate crimes, by people who 'found out the laws of living together / In cities'. Nobody would dream of pointing the finger at the mysterious meteorite which made dinosaurs extinct. Beavers ravage forests and dam rivers, but they are hardly 'responsible'. Political ecology is a type of humanism because it recognizes a moral dimension, to be approved or condemned, in the actions of a particular species. For ecologists, therefore, human beings are in a double sense 'at the centre of nature':

• It is only because humanity is both cause and victim that changes to our planet concern ecology, rather than geology.
• Human consciousness, power and responsibility make these changes a matter of morality and politics. A choice of

'good or evil ways', as Sophocles said: in any event, a choice needing careful thought.

The impasse of productivisms

From this point of view, it has to be admitted that Fordism, and the liberal-productivism which would like to supplant it, were 'bad choices'. Liberal-productivism is certainly the worse one, since by definition it is liberal, and accepts no self-limitation in the name of the collective interest, or of the right of future generations to the common heritage of humanity – a planet where they can live. Fordism, however, was also a 'productivism'.

The logic of a capitalist regime of accumulation founded on intensive growth and mass production for mass consumption is to 'produce' to the maximum and stimulate consumption to the maximum. This is simply a basic trend in capitalism, amplified in this kind of regime, for which mass consumption is the main outlet. It also appeared in those Eastern countries (sometimes called state capitalisms) where the maximum accumulation of the means of production was the driving force of the system. All production, of course, involves a transformation of the environment – either the natural one (oceans, subsoil, atmosphere) or the one previously created by humans (the rural or urban environment).

However, since neither of these environments has to be paid for, the natural tendency of firms is to deplete their resources or overwhelm them with waste. The state can choose to make firms 'reinstate' what they despoil, but only if public opinion is behind such a move. Firms are not necessarily against this obligation on principle, provided it applies to all, like keeping to collective agreements. They simply pass on to the customer the cost of the 'reinstatement'.

During the golden age of Fordism, there was no question of paying that cost – nobody was prepared to pay more for welfare in order to put right the damage caused by production or consumption, often thousands of miles away, or many years previously when people were unaware of it. By the early 1970s, however, social movements spawned by the revolts of the late 1960s began to take the problem on board. In the United States and many European countries, they managed to get ecological laws and regulations introduced, which automatically, though marginally, increased the cost of goods produced. The logic of Fordism, even when influenced by ecological concerns, is implacable – it is better to set about repairing any damage (thus boosting consumption) than not to pollute in the first place.

However, the cost of reducing pollution, when added to production costs, aggravates the 'supply-side crisis'. At a time when the share-out of value added between wages and profits becomes more problematical, the cost of repairing environmental damage imposes (or so it seems) an extra burden, an unaffordable luxury in a period of crisis and unemployment. It amounts to having to choose between jobs and ecology. This absurd dilemma was a significant and lasting factor in the divisions among the new social movements – divisions which favoured liberal-productivism. The result was that in the 1980s the absurdities of liberal-productivism, by breaking free of all constraint, caused the cup, generously provided by nature for us to dump our waste, to spill over . . .

There was indeed no constraint; everything was directed to jobs, to increasing the consumption of the 'winners', to the feast from which the marginalized got a few crumbs. It mattered not that neon signs used electricity, derived from fossil fuels wrenched from the earth to be burned, to saturate the atmosphere with emissions of carbon gases, sulphureous compounds, methane and nitrous oxide. Or that nuclear power stations produced radioactive waste which future generations will not know what to do with, if indeed the reactors themselves have not exploded before then. Or that golden boys and computer analysts were persuaded to change their after-shave by offering them aerosols with CFCs harmful to the ozone layer. Everything was directed to exports, and too bad if on the outskirts of São Paulo there is a desperate pile of human beings living on a pool of fuel oil, surrounded by glue fumes, metal dust and gases from steam crackers. Or if the soil is depleted by soya and sugar cane after staple food crops and small farmers have been displaced. Or if burning land in the Amazon sends carbon gases into an atmosphere already saturated by cars and factories in the North. After us, let the heavens fall! Or, as Keynes said, 'In the long run, we are all dead.'

The trouble is that Keynes is dead, and it is we who are caught up in the long run. Like financial debt, ecological debt has to be paid one day, the difference being that it cannot be rescheduled. We have acid rain killing off forests, a hole in the ozone layer which protects the earth from ultraviolet rays, combustion gases causing global warming, desertification, melting icecaps, rising sea levels threatening Venice and Bangladesh. And all this within the next half century. Children born today will have their skin burnt by ultraviolet rays at sea level, will see coastal plains disappear under water and crops swallowed by the desert. We may feel like saying 'If it goes on like this . . .', but we are frightened that the answer will be 'No, there's nothing we can do, it's too late.'

The seriousness of the impasse should not be under-estimated. It is not a matter of an unfortunate technical decision. The risks in producing energy from fossil fuels (more than that – the certain catastrophe) led to the rise of a lobby for nuclear energy, claiming it gave off no gases. Chernobyl, however, reminded us of the enormous risks in nuclear technology – few accidents, but dire consequences when one did happen (evacuation of a large area, enormous fallout). Moreover, nuclear energy supplies 'only' 6 per cent of the world's energy; how many Chernobyls and Three Mile Islands would there be if nuclear energy were the main source?

The finger should not be pointed, either, at specific defects of particular human organizations. After the Bhopal chemical accident, people said 'Well, it's the Third World . . .'; after Seveso, they said 'Italy . . . weak governments . . .'; after Chernobyl, 'There's Soviet bureaucracy for you.' What do they say when the Sandoz factory in Basle kills off the Rhine? A Swiss firm . . . ? The country of precision watches and direct democracy?

In fact, as productivism spread throughout our planet by imitation or the pressure of foreign debt, it saturated our ecosystem and reduced significantly the time available to adapt to the disruption which we ourselves cause. Partial solutions have proved illusory. Like a cancer which spreads, unresponsive to local remedies, the ecological crisis highlights the interconnection and interweaving of all the subsystems which the functionalist approach of productivism tried to isolate and put into separate boxes: a time for producing and a time for consuming; a time for wrecking and a time for repairing . . . Ecology, previously on the 'periphery' of the economy, is today right at the heart of the problem.

Moreover, I will not be led into saying that further progress is impossible, that human beings as the 'wonder of the universe' have encountered an insurmountable obstacle to the extension of their genius. On the contrary: the challenge that we have given ourselves is to take responsibility for the fate of the whole planet instead of building our own future on the ruins of the rest of the universe. Humanity is today clamouring for progress 'in depth': a further stage in thinking about nature, and about its organization and humanization.

It is not the first time that this has happened. In the mid-fourteenth century, the development model of European feudalism encountered this obstacle. In terms of social organization and the state of knowledge of the time, Europe was overburdened by its impoverished peasant population and had exhausted its reserves of territory. In the space of a few decades, ravaged by war, famine and plague, it lost a third of its population. After two centuries (historians speak of the 'great two-hundred-year cycle') it had reverted to its previous population level and living standards. Then, the agrarian revolution allowed this upward trend to continue: but the Sahel region of Africa never had this possibility!

Are we going to wait until AIDS, climatic catastrophes and nuclear blasts have wiped out the debt we have been contracting since the beginning of the century? Or are we going to assume our responsibilities to our environment and to future generations? At this historic 'parting of the ways', at the crossroads of the end of the twentieth century, this is what is crucially at stake.

6
Time for the Alternative

In the mid-1980s, liberal-productivism seemed to be carrying all before it. Everywhere, Fordist compromises were being rejected. The 'old' was well and truly finished. In France, the Communist Party left the government, and the new prime minister, Laurent Fabius, committed his socialist government to a form of neo-liberalism which it tried to make as human as it thought possible. The right, from former Gaullists to former Christian Democrats, sang the praises of Reaganism.

The proliferation of slogans such as '*La France qui gagne*' in the March 1986 election campaign, from the Socialist Party to the right, showed a degree of convergence round this paradigm (with its own 'left' and its own 'right', as usual). The Communist Party made clear its intention not to go along with it, though its admirable slogan, 'The important thing – don't give in', in fact offered no prospect, in that it no longer meant 'at least we will have tried' (which was the keynote of new models aspiring to hegemony), but simply the despair of 'the old that passes away'; it will disappear with the last skilled worker in the last factory in the Communist stronghold of Seine-Saint-Denis. As expected, the 1986 elections gave the right a massive victory, with 10 per cent of total votes going to the reactionary and racist extreme right. The 'moderate' right therefore felt itself able to implement fully its programme – the right-wing, explicitly Reaganist version of the liberal-productivist paradigm.

To everybody's surprise, young people – supposedly depoliticized or supporting economic liberalism ('everyone for themselves') – rose up in revolt against the right. In fact, perceptive observers would have realized the influence on young people of anti-racist movements such as '*Touche pas à mon pote*' ('Hands off my buddy') or sentiments of solidarity with the Third World in humanist songs. The arbitrary imposition of selection for entrance to higher education brought a million young people on to the streets in November 1986 calling for 'equality'. The Chirac government had to back down, not just on the higher education front but, in the wake of this, on its plans to introduce anti-immigrant and anti-drugs measures. This backdown signalled a wave of protracted and determined spontaneous strikes in the public sector, though with only moderate results because of lack of clear and precise objectives.

These revolts expressed fundamentally the same values as those of the May 1968 period: autonomy and solidarity. The difference was that in 1968 the revolts were against an all-pervasive technocratic state and therefore they stressed autonomy ('responsibility for our own affairs') before solidarity; in 1986 the confrontation was with liberal-productivism, emphasizing *first* equality (against the market and economic liberalism) and *then* the call for autonomy and liberty. After all, liberal-productivism differs from the Fordist paradigm in that it is no longer an organicist design . . . though it is just as 'hierarchical' in excluding the vast majority of people from the operation of 'free entreprise'.

After this right-wing version of liberal-productivism had been stopped in its tracks, the 1988 presidential elections in France were more auspicious. The world-wide stock market crash of October 1987 highlighted the more general problems of the neo-liberal model. Nevertheless, a centrist version of liberal-productivism was the focus for a remarkable convergence of the three main candidates, Jacques

Chirac, Raymond Barre and François Mitterrand. It was as if the economy had narrowed the field of democratic choice to an automatic application of its 'immutable laws': Europe, education and training, modernization.

Of course, the most human (and the most humanist) of the candidates won, but a significant third of voters rejected this 'broad centre', and there was a high abstention rate, which grew with each subsequent election in 1988–9. An important factor was the 14.5 per cent of votes cast for Jean-Marie Le Pen, representing the party of fear and exclusion, racial hatred and irrational fantasies. The 'silence of ideologies' – that is, the passive revolution of liberal-productivism – far from being a sign of positive consent, simply expressed the lack of consensus on fundamental values, and on how to assess less important differences.

Had France become a republic of the centre? Was this the end of the French anomaly, of internal divisions? No; my view is that France was more united at the height of the Cold War in the 1950s about the basics of what it wanted. French society has become as divided between winners and outcasts as that of the United States or Britain. Electoral abstention and racism are both signs of despair about a soulless Europe, education and training with no job at the end, and modernization without meaning. 'The old is dead, the new does not manage to see the light of day', as Gramsci's well-known phrase goes, ending with 'in the half light monsters rise up.'

Faced with monsters, the only effective response is a new project, an alternative compromise which offers the divided community a future of solidarity where everyone can hope to develop, and has the room to do so, and which confronts risks and dangers without maximalism or resignation. This project, this view of the world, exists in a diffused, unsystematized state in a significant proportion of the French people. But the proponents of this kind of alternative were more divided than ever in the various elections in France in 1988 – as indeed throughout Europe since the early 1980s. Many voted for the Socialist Party ('because after all . . .'), some for the Communist Party ('because at least . . .') and a small percentage spread themselves over candidates corresponding more closely to their basic aspirations but who were unable to find a common stance – the ecologist Antoine Waechter and the (not very) 'new left' Pierre Juquin.

Since then, France has been bogged down in scandals, while the European Commission in Brussels concerns itself with the new rules of the game . . . It may even be a bonus that the new model, if any, will be European. But what determines the kind of Europe it should be? If Europe is to be the nation of the future, what determines the basis of this?

The response of social forces offering an alternative project to liberal-productivism is this: democracy, not the market. The paradox is only apparent: to favour an alternative means first and foremost that there *is* an alternative, that there *is* a choice to be made; that democracy, debate and voting are still meaningful at a time when the market and technical matters dominate; that there is quite simply something requiring choices, struggles, compromises.

Is there anything more positive? What does the alternative compromise offer to replace the old Fordist paradigm which is on its last legs, and the liberal-productivist paradigm which is trying to emerge? Rejection of technical progress, certainly not; but certainly refusal to regard this progress as a value in itself. There are three themes against which any 'progress' and any policy must be judged: *autonomy* of individuals and groups, *solidarity* between individuals and groups, and *ecology* as the guiding principle behind relations between society, the product of its activity, and its environment.

The response of the alternative compromise to the crisis of the Fordist paradigm is therefore as follows:

- transformation of work relationships, so that those who produce have greater control over their activity;
- reduction of the amount of time devoted to paid work, so that commodity relations are less important in consumption and leisure, and creativity benefits;
- systematic choice of the most ecological technologies (that is, the least wasteful of natural resources), maximum possible recycling of the by-products of human activity, and redevelopment of derelict industrial and urban land;
- less hierarchy in social relations other than wage relations, principally in terms of feminism and anti-racism;
- at national level, new forms of solidarity within society, rejecting the monetary approach in favour of subsidies for self-organized activities with an agreed social utility;
- a move towards forms of grassroots democracy which are more 'organic' and less delegative;
- replacement of unequal relations between national communities by mutually advantageous ones between communities more centred on themselves.

A basis for a possible 'alternative economy' will be developed in later chapters, though I will not deal with the form which the state might have under the alternative compromise, or with changed relations between the sexes, or with the way in which the transition will be effected between the Fordist model and the alternative one. I would like, however, to consider where the alternative would be located in the French political scene, and more generally in countries where Fordism applied.

Firstly, as a new paradigm, the alternative compromise would not be part of the left–right polarization which characterized the previous Fordist paradigm. If, in twenty or thirty years, the alternative compromise as defined

above becomes the 'dominant paradigm', determining
the pattern of political forces as the twenty-first century
unfolds, then it will have its own left, right and centre.
However, it cannot locate itself 'to the left of the left', if
this second reference to 'left' means the left of the early
1990s (or rather the left of the 1970s); that is, the left of the
Fordist compromise.

However, as a new model presented as 'progress',
the alternative compromise is heir to eighteenth-century
liberalism and nineteenth-century radicalism, and to
socialism and Communism. More fundamentally, its initial
social base will have to encompass oppressed, reviled
and exploited people who are in revolt against alienation: women, workers affected by industrial restructuring or deskilling technologies, unemployed and casual
workers, young people of various ethnic groups in cities,
small farmers burdened by debt or outside 'the system',
and so on. In this way, it is the heir to movements of
emancipation. And in this sense (the historical sense), the
alternative compromise is a 'new Left'. Because of this, it
faces problems equivalent to those which socialism and
then Communism faced in the French Third Republic.
Externally, these concern its relationship with political
forces to the left of competing paradigms – the Communist
Party to the left of the Fordist paradigm, and the Socialist
Party to the left of the liberal-productivist paradigm.
Internally, the problem is the convergence of people coming from the old-style left with those who radically reject
this left, for a whole range of different reasons. In other
words, there is a rainbow coalition of trade unionists
favouring self-management, feminists, ecologists and social
innovators.

For the reasons stated in the previous chapter, my view
is that in present-day Europe this convergence should
not be round a specific socio-economic class, but within
political ecology; not because this approach is manifested in

very effective groups in particular countries, but because it provides a framework broad enough to tackle the complex problems faced by humanity at the present time.

However, people looking for an alternative compromise are to be found in all political groups of the old and the new left. They are also to be found 'outside politics', among those who no longer believe in politics but who still want to 'do something', 'see things through', 'be responsible for their own lives'. Having listened to the views of people who want these things, and having heard their thoughts over twenty-odd years of activism for political, unionist and ecological causes, I will attempt an economically coherent synthesis in the chapters which follow. Clearly, anything new, if it emerges, will be merely a new compromise with the system's inherent tendency to avoid the traps of liberal-productivism. The real alternative at the beginning of the twenty-first century will be merely a reflection, but a real one, of their dreams, of the dream which humanity needs to know about before it can dream it fully.

To take this next step, we need to address the agenda which the crisis itself sets out: the crisis of the labour process, the crisis of the model of consumption, the crisis of the welfare state, and the crisis of international relations.

7
Towards a New Wages Pact

At the heart of the present crisis is the crisis of the labour process – the crisis of Taylorism and mechanization carried to the ultimate stage, the crisis of the paradoxical involvement of the worker. No alternative project can skirt this problem, 'cut its losses', hand over the solution of the crisis of the labour process to managers and bosses, retire into a corner and come up with new ways of living. This is mainly because paid work will, for many years to come, occupy most of the waking time of the vast majority of people. It is important to experiment, to develop other modes of living, and this will be looked at later. But if the dominant groups impose their solution in this crucial area, then the logic of this solution will come to dominate the rest of society. The crisis of the labour process is not the only challenge which the alternative has to face. The new relation between the sexes called for by the unfinished feminist revolution is another question which is just as important. However, the way the crisis of the labour process is solved will have a bearing on relations between the sexes.

Electronics and information technology are not in themselves solutions to the crisis of the labour process. As we have seen, liberal-productivism tried to exploit new technical possibilities, by propounding two models of the wage relation – 'neo-Taylorism' and the 'Californian model'. In fact, these two models amount to the application of a more general model to two different segments of wage-earners. 'Neo-Taylorism' is the elimination, as far as possible, of all subjective involvement by those manual workers whose link with the firm should be as weak as possible. The 'Californian model' is the individual negotiation of involvement by those employees who have an active role – those who are engaged at the very least in conceptual work.

Many people, including employers, have reacted to and criticized this twin model. Japanese analysts and business people have asserted authoritatively (because of their extraordinary industrial supremacy) that their forms of labour process are superior: quality circles mobilizing the skills and imagination of manual workers to improve productivity and quality control; the 'Kanban' method to involve, in real time, all staff in the management of flows within the firm, and even between firms; 'partnership' and 'strategic alliances' between firms to pool research, coordinate firms' specialisms, and so on. Sweden, Germany and northern Italy all practise variants of this new approach to industry. Italian success is due not to the myth, widely believed in France, of an underground economy producing pullovers or electro-steel without the restraints of employment legislation, but, at least in the north, to high-quality organization, usually negotiated with the unions.

On the other hand, in countries dominated by the worship of machines and hierarchy, and by contempt for line workers' skills and union demands, there are more and more reservations, again including those of employers' organizations. Many articles in the *Harvard Business School Review*, and in France the Dalle Report and the Riboud Report,[1] have attacked the 'dross of Taylorism'. Unfortunately, just as 'Fordism in a single firm' was not really viable, so the firm-by-firm negotiation of a new wages pact is rather problematical. General Motors tried to negotiate with its trade unions over the 'Saturn project', a replica of the Japanese model, but they had to trim their ambitions after some years when it proved difficult to bring it into operation. In Sweden, on the other hand, a country which has always recognized the particular interests of workers as represented by unions, and where women play a full part in economic and social life, the Volvo plant in Kalmar showed that a new grand compromise was possible, right down to workshop level.

Mention of these capitalist, and therefore productivist, success stories does not mean that I go along with reforms proposed by ruling groups: the alternative compromise is neither the Swedish model, nor (less still) the Japanese one. What is vital is that any expressed desire to help transform the real world must combine utopianism (our values, our 'compass') and realism, in the sense of a calm analysis of the possibilities. Japanese and Swedish experience shows that it is *possible* to have a labour process which is at the same time more intelligent, more efficient economically and potentially more attractive to workers. Japanese employers, by negotiating this new compromise only in major firms, have taken maximum advantage of workers' intelligence, but have conceded in return only a certain degree of job security, without significantly improving the quality of their daily lives. For vast numbers of women and for workers in smaller subcontracting firms, neo-Taylorism is still virtually dominant. In Sweden, on the other hand, the new compromise has been extended further; hence the phrase 'Kalmarian compromise'.[2]

The compromise of negotiated involvement

The 'Kalmarian model' represents a major step forward. It is the heir to a whole social democratic tradition. But it represents a compromise which is different from the old social democracy. What is negotiated collectively between unions and management (in both public and private

sectors) is nothing less than the commitment of line operatives to involve collectively their imagination, innovative
spirit, skill and experience, not only in the minute-by-
minute regulation of the labour process, but also in the
collective systemization of practical knowledge – a task
which Taylor reserved for organization and maintenance
departments.

Totally contradictory reactions to this approach
('Impossible for workers ground down by years of
Taylorism!', 'Completely utopian!', 'Complete surrender to
the employers' viewpoint!') reveal the justified fears of
exhausted trade unionists ('The men wouldn't fight for
something like that') and opposition in principle to any
debate with the 'enemy', on the part of either 'hardline
anti-capitalists' or the more arrogant among employers and
management.

It must be clearly stated that unions and workers, and
all groups hoping for a progressive alternative to the crisis
of Fordism, can and must confront this challenge and
commit themselves firmly to the anti-Taylorist revolution.
As an economist, I say that they can do it, because some
employers – those who are most likely to 'gain' – are
already working towards it, and because it is far from
an unrealistic dream. As a committed citizen, I say that
they must do it, because the new alternative is the coincidence of aspirations which have been on the boil since
May 1968 and the age-old traditions of the workers' movement, which were hidden by Fordist compromise; because
a pact for negotiated involvement would be a step on
the way towards the historic goals of workers' emancipation, towards workers becoming responsible for their
own creative activity, towards a more democratic, self-
managed society; because it seems to me unacceptable and
unrealistic to put up with heteronomous and alienated
work, in the hope that workers who do not mind being
enterprising robots for 30 or 40 hours a week will, in their

spare time, be ecologically-minded consumers or solidarity-minded citizens; because an intellectual and moral reform of the labour process model, mobilizing human intelligence to master complex processes and be responsible to the end-user, will be a step towards humanizing the human race as well as nature.

However, it will be only one step, and only a compromise. It would be totally wrong to talk of self-management, workers' power or workers' democracy. For decades, perhaps centuries, to come (André Gorz says 'for ever', but I think this is going too far!), the social labour process will take the form of commodity relations between firms whose management (even those in the state sector, or those appointed by workers) will make decisions on the basis of markets and anticipated profit, and will impose the consequences on employees whose labour they have hired. In this sense, workers will be doubly 'alienated' from their activity – they will produce for the market, under the direction of management. The free association of communities, systematically discussing what they need to produce for themselves and precisely how, will remain forever a utopian dream. However, a utopian dream is also a pointer to the way ahead, and negotiated involvement is a step in this direction. It is not workers' democracy, but this would be inconceivable on the part of those workers who were unwilling to think about the labour process.

Fine, but it is *also* a compromise. Of course all entrepreneurs and managers would like workers to involve themselves to the full for the greater glory of the firm or department. It was for political reasons that Taylorism ruled this out – at the micro-level of workshop or office, or at the macro-level of the state. Naturally, groups of workers controlling the organization of their work, active and aware of their decisive position, are inevitably led, from a position of strength, to challenge management control of their work rate, of the utility of their products, and above all of the way in which value added is shared out. And a wage-earning class conscious of its management skills might harbour political ambitions about running the company. The Taylorist movement was directed not just at the 'happy-go-lucky' approach of craft workers working at their own pace (since they were not on piecework), but also at the ambitions of a self-aware working class, at the dangerous and widespread idea in Europe from 1917 to 1936 that 'people who can run factories can run the state'.

This was perhaps the greatest success of Taylorism: when the working class lost control of productive processes, it lost all ambition to self-management. In exchange, it gained the welfare state and the consumer society. A particular brand of unionism, such as that in the French trade union *Force ouvrière*, is the present-day jealous guardian of this retrograde compromise.

When, therefore, in the name of productivity, adaptation to new technology and product quality (the concept of zero faults), employers and technostructures choose to join up again what Taylor separated, when they offer manual workers a voice in conceptual work and a responsibility in management, they ask their staff to do a more effective and complex job, and put them in a position to demand something in return.

This is perhaps the main objection (and the main obstacle) to negotiated involvement between workers and management. After virtuously rejecting the very idea of such an involvement 'because it serves the firm or the bosses', some trade unionists, realizing what a tremendous change in relative strength it would bring, changed their argument round completely, saying 'But the bosses would not accept it! It would be a complete loss of authority! We haven't the strength to impose it, but if we had, why stick to a compromise?'.

This last question should be ignored as infantile: history never progresses on the principle of all or nothing. On the other hand, the first objection creates a real problem. In countries where Fordism developed in its most cruel form, the whole employer culture, the organizational tradition and the habits of lower management militate in favour of neo-Taylorism. This explains the very frequent failure of 'quality circles', 'modular work' and other experiments in 'participatory management' in France, Britain and the United States. The only argument capable of urging higher management down the anti-Taylorist path is the success of Japanese, German or Swedish competitors who have gone down it themselves.

However, when this argument has been used by union leaders (such as those of the French CFDT) simply to urge employers to be modern and 'aware of their own interests', they have come up against a brick wall. By being more committed to managerial modernization than the employers themselves, they confused their members but gained nothing from their opponents. As Rianne Mahon has shown,[3] it was where unions were very strong and pressed their demands – the 'great spring offensives' in Japan, the DGB in West Germany, the LO in Sweden and the 'hot autumn' in Italy – that employers were forced (most of the time) into making non-Taylorist choices. In 1984, when the CFDT abandoned its memories of 1968 and even the fight for shorter working hours, and sang the praises of 'modernization', IG Metall, the German metalworking union, was campaigning on the slogan '*Mensch müss bleiben*' ('People must stay') and pressing for shorter hours without loss of pay. Today, German industry shows huge surpluses with a 37-hour week (35 from 1993) giving real wages much higher than in France . . . or Japan.

In the absence of a conscious collective struggle by workers, a majority of employers and management will go for neo-Taylorism, and a 'modernist' minority will negotiate individually, or impose, workers' involvement over the heads of the unions. Trade unions unwilling to try to get collective involvement, as well as something in return for it, because they think they are weaker than the employers, might just as well give up fighting for jobs, wages and working conditions, since they will eventually be swept aside by 'staff unions' and 'friendly organizers' negotiating directly the individual involvement of workers.

The Communist ex-journalist Michel Cardoze highlighted the difficulty of the problem.[4] At the Michelin plant in Clermont Ferrand, the management introduced quality circles and the Communist-dominated union CGT boycotted the experiment. Management was therefore able to keep for itself the gains from workers' involvement, which led a Communist activist to say indignantly in an interview with Michel Cardoze:

> Michelin is exploiting an aspiration which people have. That's how things are developing. The men want to give their opinion and say what they think. Some comrades say 'it won't last, we shouldn't go along with it'. Up till now nobody's done anything about it, we're still talking of 'Taylorism' . . . Michelin is applying socialism, but grabbing all the advantages!.

This extraordinary outburst shows that for this activist, the employers can promote 'socialism' (meaning, for him, a group of involved production staff), but keep all the profit (that is, productivity gains). And of course he is right. But when Michel Cardoze talked to activists in the Renault plant in Douai, he found a different story: they backed the idea of 'quality groups', but the management had second thoughts when they realized the extent of the compromises needing to be renegotiated: 'the quality group experiment collapsed because the men came up with ideas which were dangerous for the employers. The men all have something interesting to say about their bit . . .'

Yes, all of them no doubt . . . but perhaps not enough for

it to be something to fight for, something on which to base relations between the two sides. In France, experiments by Bernard Schwartz in job retraining (of young people, it is true) showed that the least skilled workers could become involved in mastering complex processes, provided the labour process was changed. However, as the activist at Michelin said: 'Democracy cannot be legislated for. People are not used to that. Take the Auroux laws:[5] they don't go far enough, but they're still above the average level. A perfect law could not have done better.'

This is perfectly correct. At the Renault plant in Flins, the CFDT fought for collectively negotiated involvement. Through its efforts, retraining was made available to everybody, so that in six month workers could become 'automatic machinery operators' with wages increased by almost a half. Most workers, however, did not want to 'go back to school': in fact, it was the active unionists, that is, those who were *already* 'active citizens of the firm' – even unskilled workers – who monopolized the retraining places. I knew one of them, an African. Retrained by the firm, he joined economics and management courses put on by the CFDT for works committee delegates (in accordance with the Auroux laws), and ended up by setting up his own business!

This anecdote is very significant. There is no basic difference of paradigm between the forms of 'social entrepreneurship' found, for example, in the precision engineering of Emilia-Romagna in Italy, where, as an Italian researcher joked, 'workers become bosses and bosses become workers, while remaining Communists', and collective negotiation in a large firm about the control of production management. It all depends on the context, the general direction: and this anti-Taylorist revolution will be slow, complex and diversified. Unemployed people who set up their own businesses, and union members who negotiate reorganization of a workshop, are both going down the same alternative path.

In each case, however, the paradox of the new pact is the same: it is necessary to fight to impose on the system reforms which will make it work better, but which may eventually jeopardize it, and it is necessary to fight to wrench from it something in return for involvement in its working. What, in fact, is this 'something in return'?

The dynamic stability of employment

The guarantee of a job is obviously the main compensation to be sought, as a simple logical necessity. No workers are going to cooperate in trying to obtain productivity gains, for example, if the result is that they are dismissed as surplus to requirement! This was one of the reasons why craft workers in pre-Taylorist days worked at their own rate. 'A job for life' is part of the implicit contract in large Japanese companies, and job guarantees are one of the first things looked for in the new type of contract signed by American automobile unions.

The problem is that one firm on its own cannot guarantee the same kind of job over a long period. The guarantee of a job must be understood as a dynamic guarantee, with an inter-firm dimension, and a social dimension; and this inevitably raises the question of 'mobility'.

Most workers (even in Japan and the United States!) fear any degree of mobility, not just geographic mobility but also between job specialisms. And they are right. Work, especially paid work, is only one aspect of individual and social life, and not the most important, except for a minority of managers and research staff. Friendship, love, family life, collective commitment and creative leisure activities are today the main sources of happiness. But this is taking root in material conditions: the existence of relations which are stable, and therefore connected with territory. Even a rundown industrial suburb can be one's 'own place', one's 'country' (a 'home town' in Bruce Springsteen's melancholy song): a lost paradise.

The first 'something in return', therefore, in the alternative compromise is not a 'job', but the 'right to live and work in one's own "country"'. This implies that the collective involvement of trade unions – and in fact of every citizen – extends to the creation of new jobs: going beyond the 'How to produce?' to the 'What to produce?'. Two considerations should inspire this way of looking at the dynamic guarantee of employment.

Firstly, *skills must be preserved and extended*. It is humiliating and unproductive to disregard skills acquired by workers who switch jobs. Many models of industrial restructuring, like the well-known example of Pittsburgh, are social failures: former steelworkers are pauperized, and newcomers get the new jobs in electronics. Workers should therefore be part of the decision-making process when firms change to another line of production and regions are restructured. They bring a wealth of experience to the new firms, though they may need extra skill training. The right to this extra training and to discuss the aims of any restructuring is the prerequisite of highly successful adaptations to a changing world: in fact, the only 'flexibility' worth the name.

Secondly, *real social needs must be discussed democratically*. A great temptation for unions, and for central and local government, is to 'defend jobs' by defending production. There is a valiant effort to prop up declining industries or unprofitable operations (such as a worked-out mine), and a warm welcome for a new polluting industry or a dangerous plant (such as a nuclear power station). The tendency, even the function, of unions is to defend their members' jobs, and not jobs in a future model of development! The discussion, therefore, about 'what to produce' concerns not just workers, but the whole of society. New approaches must be found.

We are back to the old theme of 'democratic planning', which is more of a question than a reply. In reality, the only way to make progress in this direction is through long experience, initially at the regional level, of citizen participation in debates on how the creation and development of jobs can best be encouraged. For example, a study weekend was held in Nantes attended by shipyard workers and small farmers to discuss restructuring – what kind of agricultural machinery to produce (most had been imported up to that time, and the market for ships had disappeared), what retraining was necessary, and so on. This is more and more like the approach of 'labour market area committees'. French traditions are not a good grounding for these approaches to the problem, but the strength of necessity is there, as is the goodwill.

Goodwill does not go far without the means to apply it. Who is to finance dynamic restructuring for a new model of development? Who pays workers to be retrained; who pays for alternative approaches and new investment? If the starting point is that the most important thing is that producer collectives do not collapse, the simplest and surest solution is to have each firm responsible for the dynamic guarantee of jobs for its own employees. Moreover, this implicit contract is the most powerful spur to intellectual, technical and commercial dynamism in firms, as the Japanese economy shows once again. Even large North American and French firms, because they are pressured by workers and local people, try to find other jobs for redundant employees. Since entrepreneurs are so proud of their role as producers of wealth and providers of jobs, let us get them to apply the 'zero redundancy' rule, and see what they make of it.

The problem, once more, is that such a rule could not apply to small firms. A dynamic region of small and medium enterprises can offer a continually increasing total number of jobs, but this does not prevent significant fluctuations in particular firms, and even their disappearance. On an even more general level, the 'zero redundancy' rule would not solve the problem of those who are already unemployed . . . particularly young people leaving school.

The dynamic guarantee of jobs can be effective only if it is *mutualized*; in other words, if the responsibility falls not on particular firms, but on all of them, in cooperation with unions, local government, local banks, and schools and colleges in the area. In the alternative world view, responsibility for jobs is the responsibility of society in general – local or regional society, for reasons of democratic effectiveness and solidarity.

I am not referring here to 'civil society'. 'Mutualization' means the pooling of resources (that is, of contributions and taxes); debate and decision making on how resources are used – in other words, extension of citizenship and increase in the economic responsibility of 'political society'. The aim of the alternative project is not, therefore, to end the welfare state, the omnipotent state (which has never existed); the objective is to end the division between 'political society' and 'civil society', the stark contrast between 'state' and 'market', where market forces make profits and create jobs, and the state then has to intervene to help out the victims. The welfare state should be replaced by a 'welfare community' – not the family, but at the very least all people in a local area, with rich regions helping poorer ones, and rich countries helping poorer ones.

Before analysing this aspect, we must look at another aspect of what is received in return for accepting the wages pact – the share-out of surpluses.

8

The Growth of Free Time

Let us look at this crucial aspect of the alternative grand compromise. Let us assume (and there is every reason to do so) that the collectively negotiated involvement of workers will solve the crisis of the labour process; that is, will raise the rate of productivity growth while curbing the costs of mechanization. Who should receive these productivity gains, and in what form? How should the fruits of the new growth be shared out? It of course goes without saying that, however attractive workers' conscious involvement in their activity is for them, and however important the achievement of a dynamic guarantee of jobs, it is always a matter, or has been up to now, of providing more for employers. A cynical view of the last chapter would give the following summary of the proposed pact: 'Workers undertake to find new occupations where they can be exploited in the cleverest and most efficient way possible.'

I have always stressed the paradox that, for employees, the new wages pact is at the same time a step forward and a compromise. What they get in return for the compromise cannot be purely qualitative (the right to a job, participation in decision making). There is no reason why workers should not benefit in some way from quantitative improvements introduced by them into their own activity. Moreover, if they were denied this right, we would be back to the old economic contradiction of liberal-productivism: with weak demand and buoyant production, the inevitable

macroeconomic result is overproduction and unemployment – unless exports rise, but who takes the extra exports?

In other words, up to now we have spoken about the
alternative labour process model (collectively negotiated
involvement) and certain aspects of the alternative mode of
regulation (a dynamic guarantee of jobs, and partnership).
We must now look at what the regime of accumulation
might be. As a committed citizen, I would say: a regime
based on the growth of free time. As an economist, I would
like first of all to define the extent of the options available.

Neither all nor nothing

In my book *L'Audace ou l'enlisement*, written at the end of
1983, I placed heavy emphasis on the 'supply-side crisis'
which had halted the policy of 'reflation through domestic
demand' followed by Pierre Mauroy's left-wing government
from May 1981 to March 1983. While severely critical of
the conclusions which Pierre Mauroy, Jacques Delors and
Edmond Maire had drawn from this failure (by introducing
what they called 'austerity'), I did stress that the problem
was real: in 1982, the *net* portion of firms' profit, whittled
away by wage costs, taxes, financial expenses and loan
repayments, was virtually nil. There was no surplus to
share out, but this did not mean that the only thing to do
was to surrender to liberal-productivism.

The five years after that were years of freeze, even net
fall, in wages, of reduced welfare benefits, and of rationalization of production. Productivity recovered through
redundancies of 'surplus staff', more mechanization and,
even in France, improvement in the labour process model,
and a corresponding fall in distributed wages, taxation of
profits, cost of borrowing and even the nation's oil bill. The
ratio of profits to GNP returned to pre-crisis levels, in
France as in most advanced capitalist countries. In one

way or other (through neo-Taylorism or 'Kalmarian' compromises), by the end of the 1980s the supply-side crisis
had subsided, and the demand-side crisis was suspended
temporarily because of the huge American deficits. But
only temporarily.

However, when firms recover, this does not always mean
the whole country recovers. This is shown by France's trade
balance and even (the shame of it!) its trade deficit in
manufactured goods. This situation (the 'Third-Worlding'
of France's international trading position) was the direct
result of choices made since the mid-1970s: recovery of
profits through the break-up of producer collectives,
insecure employment, low wages, disregard of parasitic
enrichment by the *rentier* and commercial sectors, and a
totally unrealistic franc/mark parity.

The 'external constraint' no longer justified an 'austerity'
which could not in any case circumvent it. The need to
restore to firms a margin for investment should not rule out
using profits hoarded in the years after 1983, or sharing out
equitably the hidden booty from employees' conscious
involvement. There remains of course the problem that the
French system of production is not geared to international
demand: it must be faced as such, and not by sacrificing the
employees' share, particularly that of lower-paid workers.
When, in real terms, public sector wages drop 1 per cent
and pharmacists' income rises 5 per cent per year over
four years, the 'consensus on austerity' turns out to be a
confidence trick. To maintain austerity in the face of the
bare-faced prosperity of winners in the game of 'Get rich
quick' only exacerbates tensions.

Is it therefore a 'free for all'? Of course not. There are
three possible ways of restoring to employees their fair
share of improvements in productivity:

• an increase in individual purchasing power, for the
same working hours;

- an increase in free time, with the same, or less, purchasing power;
- a greater degree of 'welfare community', and to begin with, increased solidarity with those excluded from work – the sick, the unemployed, the elderly.

And, of course, a combination of all three is possible. But in what proportion? My argument is that, in advanced capitalist countries such as France, and because one cannot have everything, the alternative model should combine the last two as its first priority.

During the 1988 French presidential election, the campaign of Pierre Juquin,[1] who started out with a great deal of sympathetic support and media attention (he was the only 'small' candidate to be given extensive television time), lost credibility by a maximalist approach which showed the inability of many of his supporters to break with the Fordist model (the 'left wing of the Fordist left'). His redistributive programme included:

- 25 per cent increase in the minimum wage;
- the 39-hour week to be cut to 35 hours for all employees, with no reduction in pay;
- a minimum social income, equal to the minimum wage.

This was sheer folly, even from an accounting point of view. Overall, it would have required the transfer to the low paid of 30 per cent of total gross wages, amounting to nearly a quarter of the national product, the major part of firms' before-tax gross margin and several times their net profit. This is on the assumption that a price freeze ensured that this total was not depleted by inflation, that cast-iron protectionism prevented the 'recovery' being overwhelmed by a flood of imports, and effective requisition measures obliged firms to meet demand even while producing at a loss. In other words, though voters were not warned, there was going to be a war economy. Even assuming that the move to a war footing did not destroy any plant (as would happen in a civil war, for example), it is clear that there would have been consternation in the ranks of political commissars and workers' councils responsible for making entrepreneurs (or newly elected top managers) invest, or simply keep the current level of production . . . at a time when distributed revenues were already eating into capital previously invested.

In short, a country such as France can certainly raise the minimum wage by 25 per cent (perhaps at the same time reducing wage spread), and it can certainly reduce the working week to 35 hours (though perhaps with *some* reduction in wages), and it can certainly guarantee income levels equal to the minimum wage (though not if this had been raised to 6,000 frs. at 1988 prices). What it cannot have is all these at the same time.

A choice is therefore necessary – firstly, not to share out everything to everybody. Low wage levels must be raised (even with reduced working time), but it does not follow that higher-paid employees should get an extra four hours of free time a week for the same wage. This must be thought about, and it means struggle and negotiation.

In *L'Audace ou l'enlisement*, I showed that without affecting the profits ratio, but provided there was agreement to raise productivity, it was quite possible to move in the space of a year to a 30-hour week paid at the rate of 37 hours *on average* (in other words, an increase in weekly minimum wage but with an equivalent reduction beyond the median wage). Such a radical measure would mean, theoretically, the end of unemployment (if all unemployed people could find work immediately, which of course is impossible), but it would impose such large wage cuts, even for those on just below average levels, that it would obviously not get the support of a majority.

There is not much point in undertaking the impossible

task of calculating a 'reasonable' weighting. Let us merely remind ourselves that West Germany introduced a slow but sure reduction in working hours, while allowing a slight increase in purchasing power. West Germany, however, was an exceptional case: with a 30 per cent fall in population per generation, demographic collapse would soon have solved the unemployment problem. Before unification in 1990, the problem was the opposite – to attract and integrate skilled immigrant workers. A gradualist strategy such as this is obviously not appropriate for a country like France, which has no hope of a spontaneous reduction in its 10 per cent or so unemployment rate.

All I will do here is simply give my reasons for advocating a system based on an increase in leisure time, and I will return in the next chapter to the 'welfare community'.

In praise of a reduction in working time

The first reason put forward, quite rightly, by those advocating reduced working time is the fight against unemployment. Although it might sound incongruous, I must emphasize this point. The fight against unemployment is crucial, and always will be. In France, people are more or less resigned to 'putting up with' unemployment at 11 per cent. Or else, when they like to make out they are tackling the 'root cause' of the problem, they say that more education and training is needed, which is never of course a bad thing. It is criminal, however, to promise young people that more education and training will get them a job. For any given level of education and training, the more a person has, the better the chance of a job; but if the level rises, this does not mean there are more jobs available. It simply means there will be better-educated unemployed people.

My fear is that this specious argument is reinforced by the proposal, outlined in the last chapter, to improve the general competitiveness of the French economy in the framework of the new wages pact. If all our competitors do the same (and several have a lead over us), there is no reason why the general volume of employment will increase. The danger then is that we find ourselves, with Kalmarian or Japanese compromises between firms and skilled workers, in the situation of the 'yeoman democracy'[2] proposed by certain American 'radicals'. Yet this 'yeoman democracy' could well coexist with the 'serfdom' of women, young people and ethnic minorities.

A real alternative compromise must face the question of unemployment as such, and a cut in working time is one of its tools. It is the 'work-sharing' dimension which provokes reservations in some people. 'What,' they say, 'are you claiming that the number of hours worked is something fixed? Surely a country can try to increase economic activity.' Later, we will look at how this can in fact be a perfectly proper aim; for now, we note that wanting to do something is not the same as succeeding in doing it. Total employment in a country is the total of jobs governed by the logic of profitability (in effect, the market sector) and of jobs to which this logic does not apply (the public sector or the substantially subsidized sector). The first category depends on the growth of domestic demand and competitiveness, and it is clear that the equilibrium position, not easy in the context of the world market, is to some degree independent of political decisions. Jobs in the public sector depend on the level of taxation acceptable to the electorate. I am in favour of a bigger 'semi-public' – that is, subsidized – sector, and I will come back to this in the next chapter. However, not all unemployment can be eliminated by this method.

Every year, and all other things being equal, the number of hours worked and paid depends on the situation of the main economic indicators. After that, it is a matter of the number of people involved in the work share-out. I do not advocate reducing the *total* number of hours worked, contrary to the belief of those who warn that 'The way out of a crisis is not to work less.' In France in the late 1980s and early 1990s, a majority worked too long, and around 10 per cent were unemployed; that is, were looking for jobs which did not exist. In the United States, the percentage of unemployed was half this figure, but the average working week was 30 hours. However, this meant that some people were 'wasting their life earning a living', and others (especially women, young people and ethnic minorities) were scraping a living from casual work, part-time jobs and seasonal employment. This is the temporal dimension of the 'two-tier' society.

Reduced working time therefore means working less so that everybody can work, or in fact, as we shall see, everybody working so that people can work less. The solution lies not only in having more part-time work for those who can afford to opt for it. It is a matter of having *normal* full-time working hours which are sufficiently well paid to give, for example, single mothers a decent standard of living, and sufficiently short to allow unemployed people to be given jobs. In the French case, calculations based on reduction of working hours during the period 1968–78 show that one hour a week less created, *all other things being equal*, 250,000 jobs over a 5-year period (since results are not visible immediately). A move from 39 to 35 hours a week would create, over 5 years, around a million jobs. While this is not enough to solve the unemployment problem, it would be an enormous step forward – about half the total problem.

The second reason for reducing working time is the tremendous increase in education and training required in a labour-process model based on conscious involvement, and in a societal paradigm of citizens who are active in their working and democratic lives. An increase in leisure is the material condition of this conception of progress, and this implies that some of the time no longer given over to work is not really 'free', but must be devoted to more training and collective negotiation. However, this 'socially con- strained' time (in that it is not supposed to be for doing nothing, which could lead to marginalization) is also for individual development, self-expression and realization of potential.

This brings us to the third, more fundamental, reason. Even time which is 'really' free, when people think they can escape from the pressure of society – 'autonomous' time – is in fact filled. Leaving aside the lowest paid, the 'Third World' within advanced capitalist countries, who certainly need a higher material standard of living (at the very least, decent housing), we see that the biggest obstacle to happiness is not a lack of 'having' but a lack of 'being'. We simply do not have the time to do everything we want. In Jacques Attali's phrase, 'we chase after props', so that we can enjoy the little extras; but we need to devote even more time to acquiring these props (a car to get us around, a hi-fi system for music, a television to watch shows). Long before the economic crisis of Fordism, when, so it seemed, to get money you simply got a job, the productivist model came up against this existentialist barrier.

We need time for love, friendship, music, the theatre; time for discovering the world. If we have no time, we offer presents, or buy things. But do we have the time to use them? How many times do we look at a photograph, listen to a particular record, watch a particular video? Even technological props to happiness no longer save us time (as cars and washing machines were supposed to do). Time is needed to use them! If we have no time, the personal computer goes into the cupboard with the skateboard. Perhaps we buy a more up-to-date version, to keep up with the Joneses . . . But are people's ears sufficiently tuned to tell the difference between a compact disc and an ordinary vinyl one?

Fourth reason: whether or not they are used, the production of these plastic or metal gadgets, which are supposed to make up for time slipping through our fingers, uses up oil or coal, scatters a few becquerels, pollutes a few beaches and clears a few forests. Like the ass's skin in Balzac's story, which shrank after each wish by its owner, each of these products depletes natural resources, and brings us nearer (perhaps past) irreversible deterioration. The Club of Rome, the ecologists' Vézelay 'Appeal' in 1988 and a whole series of meetings of experts have reminded us many times that the 'consumer society' can never be extended beyond a small privileged minority, without the rapid depletion of our ecosystem, the common habitat of humanity. Today, even the privileged among us know that this level of waste cannot continue without bringing collective disaster. We must learn to produce and consume in moderation; and if our ingenuity allows us to make up tiem in this way, let us devote this to celebration or meditation, not to 'creative destruction', or to give it its real name, 'destructive production'!

It must not be thought that what I have just said is a plea for 'zero growth'. A model of leisure growth can also include growth in global purchasing power: not only does the income of the former unemployed rise significantly, but it is vital that a reduction in working hours must not lead to a proportionate drop in wages. Time no longer given over to work must be 'compensated'; in other words, the corresponding wages must be paid in part – a proportion of 70 per cent is what I suggested earlier. This is possible because hourly productivity gains rise with shorter working hours, and also because there are more people paying social welfare contributions; also, as employment expands, fewer people receive unemployment benefits and therefore contributions fall.

In other words, productivity gains must be divided between shorter hours and an increased hourly rate of pay. If this were not so, and the work-sharing was reflected in income-sharing, than total gross wages, simply spread over a greater number of workers, would not increase to match the rise in productivity, and there would once more be a danger of overproduction.

'Compensation' for reduced working time means higher total consumption, and therefore expanding markets . . . allowing production to be increased. Is this not contradictory, given ecologists' warnings on the risks of growth? Not if the consumption model itself encourages restoration of the environment. In the same way that the agrarian revolution in modern times made land more productive by human effort, so human activity, in the form of individual purchases and local government spending, can be directed to the protection of nature, the recycling of waste, the restoration and upkeep of forests, the demolition of dreary tower blocks and their replacement by low-density residential areas which are attractive to live in and conducive to celebration and rest. *The greening of the environment*: this is where collective debate, and tax and subsidy incentives, should be directed. A further point is that housing- and associated development is consumption (and investment) of a kind less likely to draw in imports.

This in fact is the last point in my argument (and here I am speaking as an economist again): a regime of accumulation focusing on the growth of leisure is much less subject to international constraints than a regime based on consumption. When full employment is based on a measured development of trading relations and the expansion of extra-economic activities, one is less inhibited by the pressure of international competition and the continual effort to get the balance of payments right. Investing in the quality of life, and having time available for sport, art and public debate or private conversation, does not draw in imports. It is a very quiet and unprovocative protectionism; a way of returning spontaneously to a regime which is more self-focused, more amenable to the kind of regulation organized by democratic societies.

The effort needed

Children who do not like taking medicine are told 'The reason it tastes horrible is that it's good for you.' Two thousand years of Christianity have taught us that salvation is achieved through the crucifixion and through suffering. Communist governments tell their people that the hardships of 'primitive accumulation' hold the promise of a glorious tomorrow. Therefore, when I recount the glories of time freed from work, obviously doubts remain. Would that I could convince you, dear reader, my fellow creature, my companion in life (as Baudelaire said), by stressing in conclusion how a reduction in working time is a bitter potion – and therefore an effective medicine, a realistic hope of recovery.

I hope I have shown that such a regime amounts to compromises, including compromises for its beneficiaries. One cannot benefit twice from productivity gains – once by shorter hours, and once by greater purchasing power. All the less so in that the purchasing power of the lowest paid will have to be raised *as well*. The 'compensation' for hours not worked will therefore be unequal. In other words, wage differentials must be reduced. On this everybody is agreed . . . provided that the reduction starts with wage levels higher up than oneself. However, it is at a fairly low level that cuts will operate. Even if, *on average*, there is a 70 per cent compensation for the working hours 'lost', this is seen as hurting many people, including trade unionists and ecologists. Which shows that the medicine is doing us good . . .

But that is not all: new jobs created need new work-stations – fixed assets, offices, workbenches, machinery. This is why firms (and government departments) maintain an investment margin. In *L'Audace ou l'enlisement*, I showed that to provide workstations for two million unemployed, it would need five times the total annual investment of all French firms – an impossible task.

There is a solution, more economical: have several people working at one workstation, one after another; in other words, expand shift working. There is no problem for people who already work a system of three shifts a day, since adding extra shifts simply means more free time. But it would be intolerable for those who work 'normal hours' . . . unless there was a significant reduction in hours worked per day. Two 6-hour shifts a day (8 a.m. to 2 p.m., 2 p.m. to 8 p.m.) is quite tolerable, since a half-day and an evening are left free; the firm or government department can be open to the public over a longer period, and it can make more intensive use of its equipment and buildings.

However, we need to be aware of the true extent of the problem. Because of the 'change in work practices' aspect, the more widespread the reduction in working time the more acceptable it is. But in this case, the 'reduction in wages' aspect is more salient. The experience of 'small reductions' (for example, when the left-wing government cut weekly hours from 40 to 39 in 1982) and 'large reductions' (short-time working) shows that in the final analysis the second approach leads to a better outcome, because it establishes a new life-style. It is the 'horizon effect' of a cut in working time. In small doses, the disadvantages are more apparent; in large doses (leaving work an hour or two earlier, or having an extra month's holiday, or an occasional 'sabbatical year'), it opens up new horizons which, for people who have experienced them, justify financial sacrifices.

We need to mention, however, constraints affecting

employers. Some unions and politicians in France, in an effort to mollify employers, tried, in the period after 1982, to get shorter working hours introduced on a firm-by-firm basis. By the end of the 1980s, the comic (or tragic) result seemed to be a total lack of success. Why should individual employers weaken their competitiveness by reducing working time? Only perhaps to avoid the need for redundancies; or if employees accepted a pay cut for shorter working hours . . . but they are hardly likely to be happy with this.

The fact is that a reduction in working time is effective and acceptable only if it is substantial and general; that is, if it is obligatory by force of law or by a cross-sector collective agreement. It can be effective (against unemployment) only if it is substantial. It can be acceptable only if it is significantly offset by a cut in each employee's social welfare contributions . . . therefore if there is less unemployment, therefore if the cut in working time is substantial and general! However, although this reduction has to be coordinated, macroeconomically and microeconomically, and therefore must be a statutory or contractual obligation, changes in working time can only come about through long negotiations specific to each firm, or even to each department within it. This contradiction can be once again resolved by avoiding dogmatic assertions such as 'This is for the law to decide' or 'This is for collective bargaining to decide.' It is for the law to establish a timescale for cutting legal maximum working hours (with progressive reduction in overtime allowed); and it is for decentralized negotiation of agreements to decide the pace and exact details of these reductions.

In all cases, a reduction in working time implies a double compromise: between employers and employees, about the level of compensation, and between workers themselves, on changes in the wage spread and in working practices; there is even, to some extent, a compromise between people in work and the unemployed. Reduced working hours will be accepted only as an increase in leisure time, which implies a real cultural revolution.

In the Fordist model, people would say to each other: 'Ten years ago, I could not afford this make of car or a Club Méditerranée[3] holiday; ten years ago I did not have a stereo.' In the alternative compromise, people will say to each other: 'Five years ago, I could not have spent the whole of April walking in Sicily. I got home an hour too late in the evening, so I could not have learnt to play the piano, or play with my children or chat with my friends in the late afternoon. And in two years' time, I intend to take my year off and publish a book of photographs of my home town.'

9
The Welfare Community

However advanced the compromises in workshop or office, however advantageous for employees the share-out of gains from their productive efficiency (in terms of standard of living or free time), the important thing is that the alternative compromise is the exact opposite of liberal-productivism where solidarity is concerned. It was in the cause of solidarity and equality that French students rose against the Chirac government in 1986; what distinguishes the Kalmarian compromise from the Japanese 'job for life' is the existence of a 'solidarity wage', which Swedish unions defend to the hilt.

We can only move towards an ecological compromise in a society which perceives itself as a community and which refuses to abandon the marginalized. In this sense, the alternative compromise is a new organicism, just as Fordism was. Fordism had at its disposal a powerful tool of solidarity – the welfare state, social security, various welfare benefits and allowances. These have been attacked, rightly, as bureaucratic.[1] The alternative compromise must take on 'individual' aspirations to be responsible for one's affairs, to see things through to their conclusion. To establish an 'individual organicist' paradigm is the challenge facing us.

Solving the crisis of the welfare state

It is clear that the welfare state is a very powerful yet very specific form of solidarity. This is because of many factors – its emergence from a century of industrial struggle, the victory of social democracy in Europe, the response of conservative and Christian Democrat governments to macroeconomic and social imperatives, and the struggle for civil rights in Lyndon Johnson's 'great society'. Essentially, it is a form of compromise between capital and labour, in the guise of a compromise between citizens. A proportion of distributed income is deducted from the purchasing power given directly to individuals, and put in a central pool. This pool gives a cash income to those who, for 'legitimate' reasons (illness, retirement, involuntary unemployment) cannot earn a living by working. Sometimes these disbursements are in kind (medical services), sometimes in cash but for a specific purpose (child welfare benefits).

The important thing is that the Fordist norm is to earn a living from direct income, in return for work for a 'normal' employer (a firm or public service department). On the other hand, welfare benefits (except for those given for specific purposes, as we have seen) are handed out only to recipients *who are not in work*; that is, who do not earn their living normally. The bizarre nature of this rule is not apparent so long as those in receipt of benefit are only a small proportion of the population, or when the 'non-worker's wage' is legitimate, as in the case of retired people, who think they are simply receiving repayment of savings (though from a macroeconomic point of view this is not strictly correct, even in the case of capitalization schemes). However, this norm has consequences which are schizophrenic, even Kafkaesque, for those people in work as well as non-working people.

Those in work, employers as well as employees, pay taxes and contributions to the welfare state to replenish the 'pool'. When contributions are too high (recession, mounting unemployment, reduction in number of contributors), these people start to protest, saying that they are paying for the 'lazy' ones who do not work. In fact, the latter would like to work, but they cannot find paid work, and they cannot work so long as they are in receipt of benefit. Moreover, they have to meet the psychological cost of this illogicality. If they have no job, they feel like social outcasts or dependent children. If they are doing odd jobs in the neighbourhood or moonlighting while drawing benefit, they are regarded as scroungers and criminals, and can be prosecuted and have their benefits stopped.

Apart from the (usually unfair and absurd) jibe about 'laziness', neo-liberals criticize the welfare state from a microeconomic standpoint: 'If there was no tax take, or a lower one, by the welfare state from the income of those in work, total labour costs would be lower; and employers could create lots of new jobs.' This is perhaps true for the individual firm, but applying this axiom more widely is an optical illusion. If there was no tax take, there would be no social security transfers. People losing their jobs would no longer be consumers; the market would contract, more employees (however low their cost) would lose their jobs, and so on. This old-style mode of regulation is more unstable than Fordism. There was a real-life example in the 1930s crisis: double-figure unemployment rates appeared after only nine months. With the present crisis of Fordism, it took around ten years to reach this unfortunate level.

Fortunately, neo-liberals never quite achieved their aims in this respect, either in the United States, France or Britain, because citizens did not accept the dismantling of the welfare state. Even right-wing voters and politicians reintroduced at local or regional level some of the things abolished by central government. On this score, the alternative compromise continues the whole social democratic heritage, and attempts to improve it further while at the same time taking account of criticism levelled against it.

In the most radical version of this alternative, solidarity is consolidated by the introduction of a 'universal basic allowance' (UBA), to which all members of the community would be unconditionally entitled. All other income (for example, from work) would be in addition to this basic allowance. This is the opposite of substitution payments, such as unemployment benefit, which are paid when there is no other income, or supplementary payments, paid in addition to other income in certain circumstances – a version of this called the *revenu minimum d'insertion* (RMI) was introduced in France by the Rocard government in 1988. The basic allowance needs to be high enough to live decently, even when not in work; it represents, there-fore, the optimum in solidarity and lays the foundation for a non-productivist way of life.

At an even more fundamental level, the argument put forward by, for example, the Fourier Collective in Belgium and by André Gorz[2] is that the basic allowance transforms social achievements into a basic human right, and that it is an economic necessity. I fully endorse the first claim, but have doubts about its proving that it is an economic necessity, and about the definition of basic human rights which is implied. Let us examine these points more closely.

In essence, a universal basic allowance is a utopia; this should be understood not just as a desirable state of affairs, but in a sense which I have used before – as a compass, a pointer to the path to take. It is the affirmation, in the midst of a worldly existence, of a superior right to fight for, so that it becomes a worldly right. It is the affirmation that human beings have the right to live, precisely because they are human beings, and not because they are old, or mothers of families, or because they have paid contributions; because humanity and society recognizes that its members have the specific right to life, to a life like other people's. It is an act of recognition, not of charity.

On this point, I fully agree. However, which society or collectivity is to accord this right? The nation? And to whom? To every immigrant who turns up? Europe? But which Europe? Europe including Morocco and Turkey, candidates for EEC membership? Why not all the Third World? In reality, the universal basic allowance is feasible only in a political set-up with the same values and roughly the same way of life throughout. It assumes a general compromise not just between social classes but between the unemployed and those in work within each social class – a compromise particularly about the right income level for people not in work, in the light of their previous contribution to society and their objective difficulties concerning work. A compromise of this kind requires a synthesis at state level. At any point in time, it would be different according to nation, or group of nations.

This in fact is the first economic constraint – since only the productive sector of the economy finances the universal basic allowance of non-producers, end-product costs combine those of both working and non-working population. The advocates of a basic allowance think that this is not important, because productivity gains offset these extra costs. This is incorrect, as we shall see; but even if it were true, it would not prevent, at the international level, countries with the allowance from losing their competitiveness to countries without. On this level, the universal allowance is incompatible with free trade. To get round this problem, where there was an area guaranteeing a particular level of allowance (for example, France, or Europe), it would have to be financed in a way which was neutral for product prices; that is, by a universal tax. For external trade, the cost of the allowance would have to be deducted from export prices and added to import prices, through a value added tax at the frontier.

There remains the basic economic problem: is the universal basic allowance compatible with capitalism in its present form? Its advocates see in it a weapon to combat the crisis – by creating an unconditional purchasing power, it would be the only way of absorbing higher social productivity. However, although this argument was valid for the 1930 crisis of underconsumption, the crisis which started at the end of the 1960s is not essentially a crisis of overproduction, but a crisis of inadequate profitability – insufficient productivity gains for continually increasing capital costs per head. The anti-Taylorist revolution outlined in previous chapters tries to solve this problem; but it cannot do it in a short time, and the extension of solidarity is a pressing need.

We now come to a basic problem with the universal basic allowance:

• either it is too low to allow a dignified standard of living, so that people have to take casual jobs, moonlight and so on. It then becomes a kind of subsidy to employers who, according to need, can take on people from a pool of unemployed just kept at subsistence level between temporary jobs;
• or it is fairly high, near the minimum wage, and deters people from working except, for example, managers in high-income jobs.

Advocates of a universal allowance would reply that work ought to be a right, not a duty. These are fine words. It should indeed be a right, but unemployed people on benefit and unable to find work know that it is not the case. Moreover, benefits and allowances for some inevitably mean that others *must* work for them.

Let us take the example of an automatic allowance for 55 million people in France (French nationals and immigrants) of the order of 2,500 frs. a month, depending on family circumstances. This puts on to the market 1,650 billion frs. a year, a third of the gross national product. For this, we need the corresponding *commodities* – not services of a community nature, not family support schemes, but commodities. Who produces these? Those who want to. Every economic study looking at a non-deductible universal allowance has shown that its superiority (over unemployment benefit which is lost when there is income from employment) lies in the fact that in reality it encourages people to work as well, *in order to earn money*. There is no threshold effect, unlike benefit payments which stop as soon as there is income from employment. In other words, effort pays dividends! Of course this relies on there being enough 'utilitarians' to produce, in their desire to consume, the surpluses which will go to 'anti-utilitarians' content to live on their basic allowance. This dichotomy between the 'wise' and the blind, who would satisfy their greed for consumption by paying the former a wisdom allowance, is rather improbable, but at least one can dream. One could also let a religious order gain salvation by producing the 1,650 million frs. worth of goods for people receiving the universal allowance!

To be serious, however: to get low-paid workers to produce for those receiving the allowance but not working, the universal allowance needs to be at least a third less than the minimum payment for any work (it should be understood in the following discussion that the allowance of those in work is paid directly by their employers as part of their wages). An increase in universal allowance would then be a spur to make employers improve low wages! But in any event, the universal allowance would be accepted only if people in work are sure of the social justification of allowances paid to the non-working population. There is no problem with retirement pensions and sickness and maternity benefit – contributors feel they are contributing for themselves, whatever the scheme, and of course it is not a universal allowance but a personalized one related to contribution and 'normal' income levels. The question arises only in the case of unemployed people. The conclusion is therefore that a universal allowance of around two thirds of minimum wage would be acceptable only if it meant that those who received it were *prepared* to show their solidarity with society, which is paying them. It is up to society to give them the chance to do so!

In fact, this is precisely what the vast majority of unemployed people want. A permanent state of affairs where some people are helped to do nothing is not only provocative to people in work, it is also psychologically painful for those who are being helped. Human beings do not work just for money, but for independence and social recognition. A universal allowance given only in the form of money, without society providing the means to participate in working in the community, would almost inevitably lead to people seeking extra income from casual employment; or it would operate once again as a subsidy to employers, or as a 'child-rearing wage' excluding women from socialized work.

A socially useful third sector

It is feasible to extend solidarity by a universal allowance, and cater for the criticism levelled against it, by *creating a new sector of activity* limited to some 10 per cent of the labour force, roughly the same as the unemployment rate at the beginning of the 1990s. Workers in this sector, or rather the organizations which would pay them, would continue to receive from the state money equivalent to unemployment benefits, or at least the universal allowance, and would not pay higher contributions than unemployed people do now. There would therefore be no financial implications for the welfare state. Workers in this sector would receive a normal wage, in the context of normal social legislation, from what could be called *intermediate agencies for socially useful schemes*. Their work, financially supported in this way, would centre on socially useful activities:

● those now provided at a high cost (because they are not subsidized) by certain sectors of the welfare state; for example, basic medical care or care for convalescents;
● those now provided by women, for nothing and without their having a say in the matter;
● those which are provided infrequently or not at all because they are too expensive (improvement of the environment, particularly in deprived areas, and cultural provision).

In fact, since this 'socially useful third sector' would be subsidized and untaxed, it would cost relatively little, and could open up new areas of activity. In the case of workers on the minimum wage, their costs to an employer are actually 75 per cent higher than that wage, because of social security contributions and other taxes. If unemployed people on the universal allowance of two thirds the minimum wage keep this when they get a job, and do not pay contributions, there are no financial implications for the state. However, it only costs the 'intermediate agencies' the missing third to bring them up to minimum wage level, thus opening up a wide range of possible activities at present not financially feasible.

From the social point of view, the position is more complicated. Neo-liberals are not against the idea of making subsidized workers available to firms. Because of this, the socially useful third sector needs to be strictly limited, otherwise it may destabilize everything else. It cannot, for example, include allowances in the guise of initial training schemes in private firms, favoured by French employers and the right wing, and aimed at reducing the wage costs of certain workers in the private sector. After a time, people on these courses would replace 'normal' workers, and there would be nobody to finance the welfare state. The French experience in 1987 was that, out of 660,000 such people available to employers at minimal cost, many simply replaced 'normal' workers, who were made redundant. It has been claimed that the net effect was to create or save only 133,000 jobs.[3] The proposed third sector should affect only domestic work, moonlighting, and anything which is done infrequently or not at all – prevention of forest fires, regular maintenance of subsidized housing, home help for convalescents and old people, local musical activities etc.

Here we are up against the problem of competition between the 'third sector' and the two others – private and public. It is clear that the universal allowance, paid for by taxes, and unemployment benefit, financed by contributions as 'unemployment insurance', should be paid in addition to direct wages only in the third sector, or to encourage half-time working, and that initial training schemes, where people are rented out to employers at low cost, have no part to play. Private sector employers up in arms at 'unfair competition' will have to be given proof that the third sector is not in competition with them and does not reduce the number of 'normal' jobs. If there is a 'grey area' of possible competition, this will have to be resolved by negotiation at the level, for example, of the labour market area.

An instance of this is in the maintenance of subsidized housing: public authorities cannot afford to do this, so if the third sector took it over there would be no loss to local tradespeople and contractors. The latter might in fact be given some of the work, or be taken on as technical advisors. Nowadays, only managerial and professional people can afford to have their houses painted by professional decorators, with proper billing and VAT added, and the services of the third sector would not be available to this group. What happens at present below a certain income level? People pay an odd-job person. Lower down the income scale, a relative might be called on. But what happens in the case of old women living on their own? They exist between their faded walls, they grumble about people urinating on staircases, about lifts not working; they are frightened of young people and foreigners. What a difference it would make if a team of young people from varied ethnic backgrounds came and improved their living environment! This was the 'stairwell policy' of the *Ecologie 93* list in the 1986 French legislative elections in Seine-Saint-Denis.[4] Michel Rocard adopted this slogan, though he rejected the original idea of 'intermediate firms' suggested in 1983 by Bernard Schwartz.[5]

A community-oriented third sector is therefore a way of fighting loneliness, marginalization and racism. It is a superb way of eliminating the need to moonlight. An anecdote illustrates this: an unemployed person living in Seine-Saint-Denis went to see a social worker in a municipal housing complex to try to get a job with an intermediate firm. 'What can you do?' 'I do odd jobs here and there.' 'And what are you thinking of doing now?' 'Carrying on.' 'But why join an intermediate firm?' 'Because I now have a daughter at school, and when people ask her what her dad does, I don't want her to say "He's an odd job man".'

This is a very profound reply to the inevitable question 'Wouldn't a third sector encourage a segmented society?'. There is already a segmented society – the world of unemployment, casual work, odd-jobbing, marginalization. One of every two jobstarts in France and 40 per cent of workers in Britain are part of this 'non-typical labour force'. The third sector is at least one where legal framework and wages are normal. Only the way in which it is financed (universal allowance and no taxes) makes its organizations different from private firms. This is why it has to be limited in size, just as housing subsidies are restricted to housing for the underprivileged. But the status of construction workers does not vary according to whether they are building a private block of flats or a municipal one.

A further criticism is that a third sector would be less well regarded because it would take on people not wanted by public or private sectors – unqualified women and young people, or young men with foreign-sounding names and too dark a skin. But if the alternative project does not concern itself with the marginalized, who will? Detention centres, or the Salvation Army? Obviously a third sector will start off at a disadvantage, which is one of the reasons why it will always be subsidized.

It is a problem which has beset experiments of this kind in Belgium and Quebec, as well as the few attempts in France to set up 'intermediate firms'. First of all, it was a matter of helping new firms to get off the ground, in the hope that they could progress under their own momentum; then they were reserved for the 'socially handicapped'. In the French 'intermediate firms' of 1984 one had virtually to be a one-armed, illiterate ex-convict, as well as young, to participate in these experiments. And then people were surprised that they failed!

The third sector has what it takes to endure; financial help on a permanent basis, to produce goods and provide services which are not profitable by normal capitalist standards. It is fitted to play a social integration role and take on social outcasts, though not exclusively, since it can change marginalized people into fully fledged citizens. The third sector will have its 'successes', its permanent staff and its home-grown intellectuals. I even think that it will succeed where the education system has failed – in integrating and giving another chance to the children of immigrants and to marginalized young people. This has already happened: there is a greater proportion of young people of Arab descent in voluntary community work than in the population as a whole, just as the children of peasants were overrepresented in primary school teaching in the French Third Republic.

It might be asked why the third sector could not be made into a public service department; it is not only for money reasons, since there are already too many 'civil servants' and taxes. The public service is financed entirely by public funds, by taxes. It provides services for all, according to a plan drawn up by the local or national executive. The private sector, on the other hand, provides trading services for customers. Between the plan and the market, the third sector occupies, obviously, an intermediate place. It is partly subsidized to ensure its 'right to exist', but it makes up the rest by charging its customers. It therefore has to convince its direct beneficiaries that what it provides is socially useful. Between the plan and the market, there is not 'nothing', as Michel Rocard said. There is room for *contract*, covering both a lump sum grant for work the details of which are unspecified, and detailed one-to-one negotiations on precise points.

Here we are at the very heart of the debate – the *nature of the wage relation* which will be developed. There is a fundamental difference between the neo-liberal approach (for example, initial training schemes) and that of the alternatives. Let us be quite clear: the former did not invent the 'segmented society' – it was already in existence. They simply made it official, by promising three million unemployed and 'discouraged' people a future as stand-ins, factotums and drudges, on whom employers pay no taxes and contributions.

The alternative project offers something totally different. Workers in the third sector combine in self-governed agencies, perhaps advised by management panels and professional training agencies. They make contracts with groups of end-users, local government, regional sickness insurance funds, agencies for energy efficiency, and so on. Under the contract, these customers pay the intermediate agencies sums of money which are added to the universal allowance to give members a normal wage. The quality of the service provided is assessed periodically by the two parties to the contract. It is not a matter of the bureaucratic abolition of commodity relations, but a situation where commodity relations give way to contractual and partnership relations.

In summary, the development of the third sector based on social utility eliminates most of the defects of the welfare state. The 'schizophrenia' criticism disappears. Employed people in the first two sectors (public and private) who pay social welfare contributions know what they are paying for – jobs done which are socially useful. People employed in the third sector are doing a job more highly recognized by society and more gratifying than moonlighting and odd jobs. It is in keeping with the micro-economy in that the jobs it creates are inexpensive for the bodies putting up the money, but ensure a stable income for employed people who are not in competition with other members of the labour force (unlike the position with initial training schemes). This new economic sector also involves experiments with new social relations. Internally, the sector is organized in small self-managed cooperative agencies; advised by psycho-sociologists and training staff, it can combine both training and employment activity. In its relations with end-users it can be innovative in seeking new relationships for the provision of services which are neither commercial, nor patriarchal, nor administrative, but *contractual*, with permanent democratic control by customers to ensure that the activities of the cooperatives are really 'socially useful'.

In this way, the new sector could be a learning process for self-management, equality of the sexes and democracy in the area of job specification. Although part and parcel of the market and of wage relations (though protected by its link with the welfare state), it could be a further step in the humanization of economic relations.

This is why employers are so deeply hostile to this third sector, arguing that young people in subsidized jobs should be subject to their authority, discipline and ways of thinking. However, it is not so much a matter of competition in the market for goods and services, but of competition in the labour market, competition between different sets of social relations. Young people who have gone through the learning process of self-management, of service to the community, if they transferred to the private or public sector, would be less willing to accept a mere stand-in job, the routine of regulations, or being kept in the dark about the end-value of their efforts.

Initiative and solidarity: the community synthesis

From the starting point of a universal basic allowance, we went on to look at direct contracts between intermediate agencies and their customers – from abstract considerations to the most concrete practicality. Discussion of the universal allowance involved consideration of its scope – the nation, Europe or even wider. To avoid economic distortion ('social dumping', as it is called), social welfare financing should be the equal responsibility of all competitors. We even mentioned the possibility of levying VAT at the frontier to prevent distortions spreading beyond a particular democratic community which determines a particular level of allowance and has to finance it. In the nature of things, the financial mechanisms of a general system of social welfare are abstract, technocratic and bureaucratic, even if the principle is left to democratic representation.

With Fordism, the profits and benefits of the welfare

state were shared out in a way which was just as abstract, anonymous, formalistic and bureaucratic. In France, union management of bodies responsible for social security solved nothing (this was a spectacular form of 'class collaboration' by which the *Force ouvrière* trade union in effect became the state in its most unsympathetic function – assessment of rights). For contributors and recipients alike, this abstract providence gradually became a cantankerous and wasteful milch cow, rendering people helpless and stifling initiative.

Great Britain, the founder of social security, was the first to elect to power an ardent proponent of individualism, in Margaret Thatcher. The Fordist left disappeared because it did not give to solidarity the flame of initiative, the warmth of practicality. It went to thinking that it could impose solidarity on capitalism from the top downwards, exclusively through the state. It failed to take account of the importance of workers' and citizens' sense of initiative; it discovered a taste for autonomy, only to hand it over to the firm. In present circumstances, it finds it impossible to conceive of solidarity other than from an administrative point of view, or of initiative other than as free enterprise.

It is not a simple matter to conceive of a new alliance between initiative and solidarity, something which even seems contradictory. It assumes face-to-face contact and negotiation at the basic level. In other words, it stresses the local dimension, a direct confrontation between, on the one hand, resources, skills, a spirit of initiative and imagination, and, on the other hand, a whole list of unsatisfied needs and necessary compromises. This means that people sit round a table and declare interests which are sometimes at odds with each other. The option of saying that more money should be spent or somebody should be made to pay is no longer available, because it is clear what the sacrifices are, and the mutual benefits. It can no longer be a matter of indifference that factories create jobs but pollute rivers, or that tractor-intensive agriculture leads to the disappearance of hedgerows. Material and human reality is weighed in the balance of monetary flows. Instead of a money economy, there is a global ecology, in a rural as well as an urban setting. In the most tangible sense, the welfare collectivity becomes the welfare community.

It must be stressed, however, that local development is not a paradise of brotherly love. There will still be conflicts, but the mutual interest in moving forward is no longer submerged in the hollow rhetoric of the 'collective interest'. The fight for equality and justice is more dogged, and people will say to others 'Today, you're getting more out of it than I am, but I benefit as well; and tomorrow, I will remind you that you need me.' There is no longer a 'great beyond' (the state) where all accounts are settled. There is awareness on the part of everyone that contempt for others does not pay. There will be a gradual move from awareness of interest to true solidarity – the realization that one's well-being and freedom to act depend on how far other people have freedom and success and well-being.

We have already encountered the local level, or regional level (a distinction which cannot be further developed here), when we were looking at the new wages pact, with its dynamic guarantee of jobs, and when we were stressing the decisive role of the partnership between unions, employers, local government and local training schemes. To the network of firms helping each other on the local level, supported by people demanding something in return in terms of jobs and respect for ecological norms, we than added 'intermediate agencies', collectively serving the local people. Moreover, there is no great gulf between these agencies and private firms based on local initiative which have been started up with help from local people. Individuals can change sector, just as agencies promoting socially useful work which then become profitable in a particular 'niche' can be transformed into private, non-subsidized firms. As Jacques Delors rightly said: 'Local initiative can ensure in practical terms the osmosis between the commodity sphere and the embryonic third sector.'[6]

The new, alternative model shows itself to full advantage with the change it brings to social solidarity. Fordist solidarity, organized by the state, was strictly monetary, and excluded initiative as a matter of course: a person who was ill and in a state of anxiety would in effect be given money to go to the doctor; somebody too poor to refurbish their accommodation would be told to wait until they received a grant to get it done; unemployed people would be given welfare benefit. The important thing was that people in this position were told to stay put, and certainly not to bestir themselves. It is hardly surprising that the system is in crisis!

Against liberal-productivism, the new alliance does not give an inch as far as solidarity is concerned. Yet, it is perfectly normal to pay contributions so that people are cared for, are adequately housed and can live decently even when they have no job. But the new logic encourages the use of money from solidarity to make it multiply in socially useful tasks: paying unemployed people, or rather giving financial help to self-managed agencies of unemployed people, to rehabilitate rundown social housing, enhance and enrich the environment, and help people in their own homes. These socially useful activities, mobilized against the crisis of the welfare state, ensure that any reduction in state commitment is not made good, as is usually the case, simply by the unpaid work of women.

Who, however, defines social utility? Who fixes its area of operation, so that firms in the third sector do not impinge on non-subsidized activities? Answer – customers and local organizations. The radical reform of the welfare state will be a resolutely decentralized reform in terms of management, even though the financial aspects will still have to be on a higher, national level.

There will still be risks for intermediate agencies:

cobbling together schemes merely to survive; shortage of money to fund initiative; competition from other regions; the temptation to revert to begging for help. Solidarity and local initiative can develop only by extending their horizon to the whole world, and first of all to the location of the social contract where the ground rules are drawn up – the nation-state (perhaps extended Europe-wide). Collective agreements, working hours, tax levels and share-out of 'heavyweight' public services all need to be negotiated above the local level. For the moment this is the national level; tomorrow it may perhaps be Europe, not forgetting co-development agreements with the Third World. Without these supra-regional levels to establish ground rules, there is a great danger that regions will find themselves in 'free competition' with each other to the disadvantage of the worse-off. There can be no local solidarity without national and international solidarity.

The hierarchy, however, is turned round. Change at the bottom is no longer expected to come about through change at the top. Change at the top is called for to consolidate and develop the achievements of initiatives at the bottom. As one of the leaders of local initiatives to revive the Rustbelt of north-east America said, 'Perhaps we will be swept aside by economic forces outside our control. But in any event, what we are attempting seems to me to be the only honourable thing to do in the circumstances.'[7]

10
A Non-aggressive International Economic Order

On the assumption, dear reader, that you have found my proposals both attractive and not totally unrealistic, you will probably nevertheless say 'All that is fine, but a nation adopting this model runs the risk of grave problems in the world economic struggle. How can a country where the working week is 30 or 35 hours compete with South Korea? Moreover, a democratic South Korea can quite legitimately decide to work relentlessly to improve its standard of living.'

This is perfectly true. We have already said that 'grand compromises' need not be the same in each country. The compromise which I am proposing is not even the only possible progressive compromise, and many countries will stick to the liberal-productivist model. What must be found, therefore, is an international diplomatic agreement, a 'new international economic order', to give countries which want it the best possible national compromise in the light of the situation and preferences of their people. In other words, a 'non-constraining economic order' . . . except where, in certain cases, it might constrain certain countries from being aggressive.

The main problem is that at the present time, in the neo-liberal context, the cost of 'adjustment' (that is, bringing trade and capital flows back into balance) falls on countries in deficit, which in general are those in need of economic growth to improve the lot of their people. Not only is it very serious for them, but this game of 'competitive stagnation' (reducing one's purchasing power below that of competitors) ends up by harming countries in surplus when their customers become poorer. Only the United States, with the dollar's privileged status, can escape 'adjustment' for a time.

This situation is further aggravated by the burden of accumulated debt. A country in debt must not only import less than it exports, but it must have a trade surplus to pay off a debt that it has already cleared many times but which increases with added interest as it is being paid off. Brazil was very rarely in deficit in the 1970s, and nearly always in surplus in the 1980s – its 1988 surplus was $14 billion, the world's third largest after Japan and Germany. Yet it cannot clear its debts. The frantic search for exports condemns it to the worst kind of productivism, with no growth in living standards or welfare for its downtrodden peasants and shanty-town dwellers, and with no respect for its environment.

The debt repayment time bomb

This is a perfect example of a global order which restricts the choice of development model to one which is productivist, non-egalitarian and rapacious. However, the pursuit of growth on credit in the 1970s (extended into the 1980s in the United States) merely leads to an accumulation of threats. To attract loans, debtor countries have to raise the interest rates on offer, so that capitalists see more advantage in speculating than in engaging in productive activities. This became intolerable for the Third World, and it is becoming so for the United States. The time bomb of debt could explode any time, when creditors refuse to go on lending, and the result would be international chaos of such proportions that it would be very difficult to re-establish, at national level, a satisfactory development model.

The short-sighted solution is to call for a rapid return to a situation where national accounts were in balance, saying in effect 'If the Third World and the United States stopped living beyond their means and repaid their debts, interest rates would come down and general economic recovery would be just around the corner.' However, this fails to take account of the present state of the crisis. Firms have reached a satisfactory level of potential profitability. The bottleneck is now entirely on the demand side – the extensive rights over future production which creditors have accumulated are going to force most of the world (the Third World and the United States) into policies of austerity, and these, by dragging the world economy into an implacable recession, will simply make repayment of debt impossible. This can be explained as follows.

In an article published in 1984,[1] C. Jedlicki calculated that the Third World, to clear its debt (then standing at $600 billion), would need a net export surplus of $124 billion a year. This was equal to the total annual American trade deficit, which would have had to be devoted entirely to Third World exports. This of course did not happen, fortunately for Europe and Japan. At the end of the 1980s, Third World debt was more than $1,300 billion, and United States foreign debt was set to overtake this figure in 5 years. This double debt became intolerable for the world financial system, but its repayment (at the cost of draconian austerity policies in the United States and the Third World) would mean that Europe and Japan would have to agree to a deficit of several hundred billion dollars a year with the rest of the world. The result would be disastrous for jobs, since Japanese and European exports would be replaced by imports, and probably irretrievable chaos.

As for the plight of debtor countries, I leave it to others to hint at what would happen, and to tell people who have not been in the streets and on the hillsides of Brazil, Peru and Mexico. Latin America alone in the space of 5 years had to transfer to the North $180 billion, or 4 per cent on average of its GDP. This is a penalty which would never have been imposed on Japan or Germany after their defeat. What Auschwitz have the Latin Americans committed to deserve this Hiroshima? What future Nuremberg Tribunal will sit in judgement on our age because we allowed this to happen?

In other words, the repayment time bomb is even more dangerous than the debt time bomb. On the grounds not only of morality, therefore, but also of the logic of the macroeconomy – looking at the problem globally, in the interest of everyone's standard of living and job, and probably of world peace – there needs to be the largest possible *devalorization* of debt. However, cancellation of international debt, already significantly under way, poses many problems.

Most importantly, the 'official' cancellation of debt poses a credibility problem for future lending, and it can be wrong to write off two similar debts which have not been put to equally good use. Human solidarity suggests that the first priority in writing off debts should be those of the poorest. Should debts owed by dictators be cancelled, or a premium be given to countries recently embracing democracy, such as Brazil or Argentina? To go to the heart of the problem, should United States debt be written off?

Of course the United States devalued their currency by half against the Deutschmark and yen in the space of two years (1985–7), thereby preserving their expansion and partly recovering their competitiveness, but also writing off half the value of their dollar debts. Third World countries have already limited their imports (with often dramatic social consequences) to such an extent that their trade balance is really only made up of demand from the developed world. For these countries the only solution is the devalorization of their debts, which is already happening in that banks sell these debts to each other on the 'grey market' at a discount.

In some governments of the 'North' such as France or Japan, and in some international organizations such as UNCTAD, an increasing number of experts and major figures, no longer voices in the wilderness, are coming out in favour of writing off debt to the fullest possible extent; that is, as far as the tolerance of other governments will allow. My conviction is that there is a hidden majority among 'elites' in the North, including the top echelons of the IMF, who would say that the massive reduction of Third World debt is inevitable. The only obstacle is that this 'hidden majority' can show themselves only if debtor nations push them into it, with the help of non-governmental organizations in the North favourable to the Third World, and of trade unions in the North who do not want to see 'repayment' take the form of massive imports.

However, this push has not yet happened, because of the inability of the 'big debtor countries' (Argentina, Brazil, Mexico, Venezuela) to coordinate their efforts and, even worse, because of a lack of conviction on the part of elites in the South. The astonishing readiness of these elites (even including the centre-left) to impose on the lower classes the repayment of a debt which they did not take on cannot be explained merely by the threat of retaliation by the lender countries – a threat which could be countered by a determined 'Debtor Nations Club'. In fact, there are in the South powerful pressure groups in whose *interest* it is to repay debts – financial intermediaries, the export sector and so on. Moreover, intellectuals (even on the left) internalize more and more the difficulties of a coordinated campaign of non-repayment. These difficulties are real, but they can be overcome if the debtor nations of the South can unite, exploit the fact of potential allies and a 'hidden majority' in the North favouring accommodation, and put forward a concrete alternative.

The problem with the official and extensive writing off of debt is of course its effect on creditors. What will happen if devalorization is extended to a dramatic fall in American Treasury bill rates, or the cancellation of Third World debt? In so far as these now worthless assets sustained the entire world banking system, the collapse of banks which made the loans and the general breakdown of the world monetary system could follow. However, a controlled reduction of bad debts *reassures* banks' customers, and it only becomes *dangerous* if it is massive and generalized. This is why Mexico was unable to exchange officially its debts, depreciated by 50 per cent, for bonds backed by the United States Federal Reserve.

The rapid devalorization of Third World debts is possible, therefore, only if a supra-national monetary body, acting as 'lender of last resort', compensates banks for debts which they write off. This body, and not the debtor nations, would pay the debts owed to the banks, with a certain amount of discount. This is a revival of 'special drawing rights' (SDRs), which are simply credit money issued by a supra-national body, the IMF. At present they depend on the amount of deposits which major countries are willing to lodge with the IMF. However, there is nothing in theory to stop the IMF acquiring the status of a world central bank, issuing paper money which is 'as good as gold'; that is, universally accepted as a means of payment. This, more-over, is what Keynes suggested at the Bretton Woods Conference which established the new international system just after the war. The proposal was rejected by the United States, which imposed the dollar as the international credit currency.

The international situation today is so tense that we need a *new Bretton Woods*. Allowing a world body such as the IMF to issue money, at interest rates independent of changes of fashion in Washington, would mean the end of many bottlenecks. These special drawing rights would first be given to banks to offset unpaid or unserviced Third World debt, then distributed annually according to the development needs of the peoples of the world. They could also be used to finance raw material stocks held to stabilize prices, the main source of income for many Third World countries.

A 'new Bretton Woods' would solve four major problems: Third World debt, raw material price stability, financing of Third World aid, and stabilization of interest rates at a reasonable level. A solution such as this would of course be camouflaged as something more orthodox – there are many proposals in the air, but on closer examination they amount more or less to the same thing. The solution would doubtless have the support of Japan (which needs customers but cannot finance a 'Marshall Plan for the Third World' by itself), and of France (though France would be opposed within Europe by conservative governments in Britain and Germany). It would strengthen the powers of the IMF or of a new international agency to manage the securities issued as a substitute for debts.

The IMF has had a bad press in the Third World. This is somewhat unfair, in that the basic principle of the IMF is sound and useful, but the policy followed by its leaders (acting as representatives of the international financial community) is reprehensible. The Peoples' Court at its meeting in Berlin in September 1988 condemned the IMF and the World Bank for not acting in accordance with the social aims of their own charters. Reform of the IMF, and its democratization by making it responsive to Third World points of view, would certainly raise enormous technical and diplomatic problems. But as the twenty-first century approaches, this is what is crucially at stake.

The United States would be the major loser. Not completely, however, in that it would recover as SDRs the Third World loans which it was resigned to writing off. Assumption by the IMF of the role of world banker would be the final blow to the hegemony of the dollar, which would lose its status of *de facto* world currency. However, could the United States have prevented this for much longer? This is the problem raised by the adjustment of its deficit.[2]

The end of American hegemony

However irritating the prospect of the United States escaping the austerity so strictly imposed by the IMF on the Third World, it does seem as though this adjustment should be made as far as possible without provoking an American recession, if only because the price of a recession would be met principally by women, black and Hispanic minorities, young people with an uncertain status, and the whole of the 'Third World' within the United States itself; and because a drop in American imports would be very serious for Europe and Japan, and dramatic for newly industrialized Third World countries, for which the United States is the main customer.

What is the way to achieve this non-recessionary re-establishment of the trade balance between the United States and the rest of the world? The United States made a first attempt by negotiating with its partners to devalue the dollar at the end of 1985. But this solution did not improve its deficit with countries in the dollar area, which led to protectionist measures against its Third World suppliers. Above all, German and Japanese lenders, worried about the devalorization of their dollar loans, became more and more demanding in terms of the interest rate they could expect on their loans. The Japanese in particular became increasingly reluctant to 'get their fingers burnt' by buying Treasury bills, and the dollar lost its function as a reserve currency.

All in all, the loss of economic hegemony by the United States and the impasse into which it was put by the two Reaganite periods implied an explicit surrender of its monetary hegemony. In its quarrel with Bonn, which triggered the October 1987 stock exchange crash, there were echoes of the British government's attacks on the 'gnomes of Zurich' when sterling was losing its dominance in the 1960s. A sinking currency cannot remain a universal currency!

However, the United States could not get back into balance by electorally unpopular austerity either. After the 1987 crash, the United States, unable to impose 'reflation' on its trading partners, hovered on the brink of further inflation and higher interest rates, leading to other serious crashes and to loss of confidence in and collapse of the bond market, then of the Tokyo stock market, and so on.

The socially and economically preferable solution would obviously be an increased level of imports by the two other economic blocs. Japan tried to stimulate domestic economic recovery, but this was not enough to solve the problem: as a middle-sized nation with an ageing population, overequipped to meet domestic demand, it will probably never be an economic bloc with high import levels. And Europe is paralysed by the contradictions of the Common Market, as will be seen in Chapter 11.

Social clauses and free trade

The cancellation of debts would sweep away the past; the universal use of SDRs as a currency would open up the possibility of development models other than export-oriented productivism. But only the possibility, in that there is nothing to prevent a particular country, North or South, from continuing to subsidize the purchasing power of its upper classes through imported goods, by obliging small farmers and workers in export industries to finance these imports. These products, sold cheaply on world markets, would establish a new norm for other countries, which would find it impossible to reconcile free trade with an alternative model within their country. In other words, the financial aspect of the reform of the world mode of regulation must be accompanied by measures to deal with the commercial aspect.

At first sight, protectionism is the best way of guaranteeing freedom of choice in the matter of a national development model. If a country has, by democratic means, reached a 'correct' internal compromise which represents the best match between the needs of the community and the wishes of its members, it should not be upset by the arbitrary working of free trade. In a situation where one or more of the more advanced countries dominate the world, every country which has become responsible for its own future has been obliged to start with a protectionist stage, whatever development model it adopted. This was seen in the economic aspects of the American War of Independence, at the start of Bismarck's Germany or in the Japanese revolution in the Meiji era; it was also how both Brazil and South Korea got their chance.

Nowadays, protectionism has its disadvantages, some of them serious. It inhibits the spread of new processes and products – and all new developments are not of course ecologically harmful. The 'economies of scale' from mass production are lost, which is not necessarily good for the growth of leisure time. Massive investments harmful to the environment have to be duplicated in several countries. Arguments such as these were influential in the setting up of the European Community to extend the Fordist productivist model.

More recently, these advantages have been cancelled out in the world trade war, which obliges countries to sacrifice everything to export capacity. The example of the EEC is particularly spectacular, and will be examined in the next chapter. What should be done between the EEC and its trading partners, and more particularly what should be done about North–South relations?

To restate the problem: to get their accounts into balance, countries have to lower their own labour costs so that their goods are more competitive and their people, because they consume less, import less. This 'beggar-my-neighbour' approach leads to general stagnation, unless certain countries borrow. How can this 'wage-cut protectionism' be prevented? Only by introducing social clauses into the ground rules of the free trade system, in the same way that collective agreements and social legislation in the national context moderate competition between firms based on the super-exploitation of workers.

Is this utopian? We merely have to look at what the Reagan administration, the champion of free trade, was saying after 1986 to its Japanese and German creditors, as it tried to right its trade balance without jeopardizing living standards and jobs in the United States: 'Stimulate growth in your own countries, otherwise we cannot stop Congress passing protectionist laws!'. Such sentiments are not very elegant or diplomatic, and they are even rather arrogant, but deep down, they reflect a perfectly correct position – that countries which sell too much must make sure they import more or export less. It is their democratic choice whether they do it by boosting domestic consumption, or by increasing leisure time, but it is not up to countries in deficit to make all the effort. If others try to make them do this, they are justified in becoming protectionist!

The diplomatic process by which this principle will be recognized will be very long. Between the major countries, it will be a matter of reason and relative power. Where the Third World is concerned, it is already extremely arbitrary.

The North puts the South in an inextricable dilemma: they are told to settle their debts, which amounts to establishing a net surplus of exports – exporting more than they import. However, faced with these massive exports by the South, the North, seeing its own small farmers and industry ruined, resorts to protectionism against its own debtors.

This is the paradox of what might be called the 'neo-mercantilism of the North'. Advanced capitalist countries were very happy to get cheap goods from the South at the end of the 1960s; the left wing referred to it as the plundering of the Third World. Now the North, through protectionism, refuses to plunder the South, in order to save its own jobs. Such a state of affairs teaches us one thing at least: the North, even Northern capitalism, is not a unified bloc or cabal of countries, capable of acting in a rational or Machiavellian fashion. All social classes are characterized by ambiguity and inconsistency:

• The North as financial capitalism is in favour of making the South repay debts; as industrial or agrarian capitalism, it is against competition from the South.
• As wage-earners, workers in the North fear competition from those in the South; as consumers, they enjoy cheap clothes, video-recorders and microwave ovens exported by the South.
• Pro-alternative activists or trade unions are against the 'plunder of the South', but are frightened of appearing to threaten jobs in the South!

The dilemma is a real one. Long discussions with unions, workers and small farmers in the South have convinced me that Northern protectionism is better for Southern workers than the horrors of the export-oriented model imposed on them, that it would be better if Southern textiles went only to people in the South, and that small-scale bean producers in Brazil – or small-scale animal breeders in Europe –

should not be threatened by Brazilian soya exports to Europe.

Freed from the constraint of debt repayment, countries in the South could choose to redirect themselves to domestic consumption. Freed from pressure from the South, Northern employers would be less inclined to 'rationalize', introduce automation, reduce wages or extend casual working. It might be asked whether goods would be dearer for consumers, but what use can unemployed people make of the freedom to consume the fruits of the super-exploitation of female workers in Thailand?

I think two rules could regulate the contradiction. First, a country with foreign debt should be allowed to restrict its repayments to a small proportion of its exports (10 per cent is the frequently quoted figure in Latin America). In this way, if protectionist measures in the North went too far, non-repayment would automatically follow. Secondly, social clauses would be imposed on the free-trade system. There would be no place for countries which were competitive through the super-exploitation of their workers, the extinction of union rights or the repression of independent unionism. These clauses would protect not just 'the North' against 'the South', but especially the more democratic countries of the South against competition from less democratic ones.

Is all this unthinkable? Then what of the following paragraph:

Ministers [of the Preparatory Committee for negotiations on multilateral trade][3] recognize that the denial of workers' rights can prevent the attainment of the objectives of GATT, and can bring about distortions of trade which then lead to protectionist pressures. Consequently, these negotiations should examine the effects of the denial of workers' rights on the contracting parties, the relationship between workers' rights and the articles and objectives of

GATT, and consider ways of tackling the problem of workers' rights in the context of GATT, in such a way as to ensure that the growth of trade relations benefits all workers in all countries.

This amendment was rejected. But who used this diplomatic-leftist jargon? The United States delegation.

'Of course,' the 'vigilant anti-imperialists' will say, 'this is the United States taking care to justify its arbitrary protectionism by social considerations!' No doubt. But in this situation, hypocrisy (the homage paid by vice to virtue) is nevertheless significant – there are powerful interests in the North that press for *not* plundering the South in conditions of too much super-exploitation. The whole question is who the judge in the matter of 'workers' rights' and 'benefit to all' will be. In my view, it could only be a supra-national body, such as the International Labour Organization in Geneva.

However, on to these abstract 'rules of the game' must be superimposed negotiated agreements between North and South, based on dynamic complementary factors and aimed at balanced relations and partnership in technology transfer – what is referred to as co-development, but which we cannot go into here.

An agency for the protection of the common heritage of humanity

The aim of all the reforms suggested above is to safeguard the freedom of peoples and nations to choose the most progressist development model possible as a function of their own democratically determined choices. But our guiding principle (that freedom to choose a development model is limited by others' freedom to do the same) has consequences which are far more constraining in at least one area – ecological problems affecting the planet as a whole.

The problem is a straightforward one, and can be broken down into a large number of specific questions. Has France the right to allow cars on its roads without catalytic converters, or Germany to allow cars, even if 50 per cent pollution controlled, to do 110 miles an hour on its motorways, when neither country can stop 'its' pollution being carried away on the winds? Has France the right to build a fast-breeder reactor, which it takes care to call experimental despite its enormous size, only a few dozen miles from the Swiss frontier? Have the countries of the North the right to wait a few more years, until the destruction of the ozone layer, before they ban aerosols containing CFCs? Has Brazil the right to burn its Amazon forest, the lungs of the planet, to avoid having to introduce agrarian reform on land already cleared?

One can have smoking compartments on trains; but there cannot be polluting compartments on our planet, especially since the effects of pollution are so complex that it is impossible to pin the costs on polluters. When rising sea levels have flooded Bangladesh, will the refugees be resettled in countries pro rata according to their contribution to the greenhouse effect which melts the icecaps? The ecological security of the planet has to be collective, and it is therefore the duty of an authoritative international agency to stop the desecration of our common heritage. It needs to be an agency with the resources to study and assess issues, independent of governments, but able to take them to the International Court at The Hague or to the Security Council if they are in breach of its directives.

Such an agency needs to have financial resources, if only to compensate countries which are denied full use of their own resources – in the same way that the compulsory purchase of property in the public interest is compensated. These could be provided by taxes levied on consumption or on the use of certain pollutants. For example, oil price rises led the whole world to adopt energy-saving policies, which could be relaxed if prices dropped sharply. A quasi-tax on fossil fuels could provide funds for the agency and at the same time deter dangerous waste by consumers.

The agency, in association with the World Health Organization and the Food and Agriculture Organization, could step in to prevent natural disasters on a world scale. Its role would be all the more decisive in that disaster prevention poses problems which are typically ecological – for example, the fight against locusts in Africa requires not only close international cooperation, but also a careful choice of pesticides. Gradually, this supra-national agency could establish its own tax system, by having the exclusive right to excess profits from inventions vital to the whole world. It is scandalous that the race to find an anti-AIDS vaccine should be hampered by sordid commercial rivalries between laboratories.

However, the agency would not necessarily always take direct action. It could encourage national measures in favour of ecology – taxing polluters, subsidizing non-polluting vehicles, saving energy, and renewable energy sources (a kilowatt-hour of energy from the French *Super-Phénix* fast-breeder reactor costs ten times more than from solar power;[4] why should there not be a world programme to develop solar technology?). To do this, it would have to cross swords with the ardent proponents of free trade, such as the European Commission, which in 1988 tried to stop the Netherlands reinforcing its anti-pollution policy.

Is it still a utopia? It amounts to the abolition of torture and chemical weapons, but the difference is that all of us are involved, all the time; and it is later than we think.

11
The Alternative: A Project for Europe

Since Fordism lost its fervour and its flair, and liberal-productivism reached an impasse, united Europe has taken on the role of the heavenly city – the mythical place where all problems vanish. In those areas where state socialism and dogmatic neo-liberalism have failed (growth and jobs), the single market of 1993 will provide the answers. This was the line taken by the three main candidates at the 1988 French presidential elections. It is not, therefore, surprising that one French person out of three voted for 'minor' candidates, or abstained. But if things go on as they are, the idea of a 'single European market' will become, like immigrants, a scapegoat . . .

Let us ignore pronouncements (which are not in any case false) such as 'The single market will harm France.' Pierre Mendès France, the champion of the 1950s modernization, was against the EEC for this reason. Charles de Gaulle, at first sceptical, was able in the end to meet the challenge. By means of an extremely goal-oriented 'developmentism', the gamble had worked by 1970; but through his successors' lack of perception, it seemed to have failed by 1980. The double switch of political power in France in the 1980s did not solve matters.[1] However, the secret of nations and regions which 'win out', such as Japan, Germany, Sweden, northern Italy, Massachusetts and Michigan, is well known – mobilization of producer skills, truces in the conflict between unions and management, partnership between goverment, research bodies and industry. Let us assume that the Mitterrand–Rocard team may have been the right one to apply this formula.

However, the question is more basic. Montesquieu said 'If I was aware of something which was useful to my country and harmful to Europe, or useful to Europe and harmful to humanity, I would consider it criminal.' The question is not whether the Common Market and the Single Act which completed it are useful to France, but whether they are useful to Europe, and whether, being useful to Europe, they are useful to humanity!

EEC-paralysis

Was the completion of the Common Market in line with the Single Act a good thing? After all, the Common Market was set up in 1958, and its advantages and draw-backs are clear. Since 1980, GDP and investment levels of all member countries have kept within a narrow band. In growth and employment, however, the EEC has lagged far behind the OECD as a whole, and particularly Japan and the United States. Growth in output between 1980 and the beginning of 1988 was 8 per cent in the EEC, as against 30 per cent in Japan and 20 per cent in the United States. Unemployment in the EEC remains at around 10 per cent (8 per cent in Germany because of demographic decline) – twice as high as in the United States and four times as high as in Japan. Euro-paralysis? Not if one looks at the six advanced non-EEC European countries – Sweden, Norway, Switzerland, Austria, Iceland and Finland – which are at Japanese levels. In the period 1980–8, growth was 40 per cent in Norway and 20 per cent in the rest of the non-EEC European countries. Apart from Austria (7.3 per cent), 1988 unemployment rates were lower than in Japan, with 0.8 per cent in Switzerland and 1.6 per cent in Sweden.

There is no Euro-paralysis, only EEC-paralysis. The Common Market is suffering from an internal regulation deficit. However, the EEC did once work well – between 1957 and 1973 each country had an identical implicit accord, varying in conflictual level, between government, employers and unions. This accord, referred to in the Treaty of Rome, implied a rapid rise in workers' standard of living which would provide an outlet for productivity gains.

There was, however, no explicit mechanism to ensure intra-Community trade balance. A more rapid rise in purchasing power in one country than in another gave rise to the double risk of a trade deficit (to which I have referred many times) – when production costs rise more quickly in that country, competitiveness decreases; and when purchasing power and investment rise more quickly in that country, with the same import coefficient, imports rise. The very principle of opening up frontiers, and pro-gressively increasing economic integration, gradually weakened the balance of payments of each separate country, particularly the less competitive and the fastest growing (often the same country). Member countries of course had three regulators. They could:

1 slow their own growth voluntarily;
2 increase competitiveness through devaluation;
3 keep non-tariff customs barriers by means of technical norms, need for approval, and the safeguard clauses provided for in the Treaty of Rome.

In the 1970s, in Europe as elsewhere, higher oil prices further boosted the internationalization of intra- and extra-Community trade. But this was the time when regulators 2 and 3 became unavailable:

● The European Monetary System forbids a country to devalue without the agreement of its partners and par-

ticularly of Germany, the *primus inter pares*, which tried to
eliminate its competitors by allowing devaluations too small
for them to re-establish competitiveness.

● The use of safeguard clauses fell into disuse, except for
southern countries such as Italy. The Single Act made the
third regulator unavailable after 1 January 1993; firstly, by
imposing open tendering and thus depriving governments
of a tool of national industrial policy; secondly, by eliminating the remaining administrative restrictions on imports
(requirement of approval etc.), thus opening up French or
Italian markets to Japanese cars, for example; and finally
by harmonizing VAT to put an end to separate national
rates.

After 1992, the only remaining regulator is the first one. To
correct its own trade balance, each country needs to grow
less quickly than its neighbour, and reduce its costs further,
by lower wage levels, less extensive reduction of working
hours, lower social welfare and less government spending.
The result is a further slowdown in domestic demand and
an increase in unemployment, affecting particularly the less
rich countries, or those expanding demographically – the
southern countries, Ireland, and also France and Italy.

It is very significant that Jacques Delors became president of the EEC Commission, in that he was the French
finance minister when the Mauroy government terminated
the 'socialist' experiment, shattering the commitment and
confidence of tens of millions of French voters and people
throughout Europe who had followed the experiment with
hope and sympathy. Delors said to the French people 'From
now on, we must try to grow 1 per cent less quickly than
our partners.' One does not need to be an expert in game
theory to guess the overall effect of twelve such strategies –
stagnation! Only coordinated action at the European level
could have countered this perverse dialectic. No doubt
Jacques Delors thought he could give impetus to this

coordination by transferring to a higher level. However, Europe was controlled by two conservative-liberal blocs – Britain and Germany.

The result was that the European Single Act, promoted by Jacques Delors to eliminate the remaining 'airlocks' and extend competitive trading without providing corresponding common socio-political mechanisms, could only aggravate the problem. The Common Market became what Michel Rocard had long thought – a free-trade zone without a common social policy. 'The common Market against Europe'.[2]

This was quickly realized by French intellectuals and employers, including long-standing champions of the European mystique – people whom I called the 'Saint-Simonians'[3] in my book *L'Audace ou l'enlisement*. This group of intellectuals, holding a pivotal position in centrist politics and the 'second left', came to power along with Michel Rocard in May 1988. But it was Rocard who uttered the first cries of alarm, triggered apparently by the debate on a wealth tax which was supposed to finance the RMI income supplement (see p. 95 – the only 'left-wing' policy proposed for Mitterrand's second presidency. In June 1988, experts pointed out that any tax on capital was circumscribed by the European context, given the imminent introduction of the free movement of capital in the EEC. On capital taxation, France ranked in the middle, and in the absence of European legislation, would have to fall in line with the country with the lowest rate – Luxemburg. In other words, to the 'least favoured working class clause' (which is what free trade amounts to) is added the 'least taxed capital clause'. This would lead ultimately to a Europe where only income from employment would be taxed!

In summer 1988, Rocard extended the debate in stark fashion, saying that a uniform European VAT rate in a single market would lead to a large fall in the revenue of countries like France, where half the budget is financed by indirect taxation. In other words, the choice was between Europe and a situation where sovereign states and their social welfare systems still had a role to play.

Edmond Maire, then the strongly pro-European leader of the CFDT trade union, used his annual August article in *Le Monde* to attack on another front: without a social policy already in place, the single market was simply going to allow 'social dumping' by countries with the most unfavourable wage relation. Maire was echoing what Michel Albert and Jean Boissonnat had said in their book *Boom, crise, krach*, published a few months earlier.[4]

Nearly all the Saint-Simon group threw off the shackles; the last of the group was Alain Minc, previously a dogmatic supporter of unrestrained neo-liberalism and European union through the market, whose book *La grande illusion* is a strong indictment of European mythology.[5] As a long and masterly restatement of the warnings which Philippe Messine, myself and others had been giving for the previous five years, Minc's book was the culmination of a salutary trend. At last the debate had begun!

As somebody who had fought to get French socialists to put progress on Europe before social objectives, Jacques Delors had to react to this attack from people whose basic outlook he shared. He wrote in *Libération* in reply to Edmond Maire that there was a need for a social Europe, and that 'we' (that is, Brussels) were applying it – see, for example, in the road transport field. He quoted his personal triumph at the 1988 Trades Union Congress when British trade unionists, reeling under ten years of Thatcherism, had come to realize that their salvation was in a Europe unified according to the norms of West Germany, the paradoxical champion of social and union rights, and the 'straggler' in the process of 'flexibilization'.[6]

The example of road transport (by its nature an internationalized activity!) is extremely interesting: over the years, German employers had to concede extensive social legislation, and this led them to seek 'virtuous' productivity gains rather than the easy solution of social regression. But this advanced compromise, which gave Germany its strength, can be destroyed if it has to compete too directly with minimally protected labour in southern Europe. It is not surprising that Germany was the first to impose social clauses on the free-trade system. German employers, however, as Zachert points out, tried to use the EEC Transport Directive (inevitably less advantageous to wage-earners than German national agreements) to harmonize, 'downwards'.

It was on the theme of monetary union that the debate became heated. Government control of credit – opening and closing the tap – is the most direct method of regulating social harmony, as was seen with the 'monetarist shocks' of the 1980s. Free movement of capital means in the short term a form of monetary union, and therefore a clear surrender of sovereignty to some kind of European central bank. The EEC's Boyer Committee was about to tackle the question when Margaret Thatcher declared provocatively in the House of Commons that 'There will be no central bank so long as this House exists.' Of course this was hyperbole, but there was a grain of truth in what she said: fixing interest rates or money supply determines the level of social tension or compromise; it is an assertion of political sovereignty which ought to be subject to democratic control.

The era of a purely techno-economic Europe is coming to an end. A decision to continue with it would be political, equivalent to bringing back the competitive jungle of the nineteenth century. The Jacques Delors tendency in the EEC Commission rejected this, which annoyed Margaret Thatcher, who regarded the Commission (in reality very circumspect people) as a 'bunch of old-fashioned Marxists'.

On the other hand, if the choice is to keep the social objectives and ecological constraints of economic activity, and to strive democratically for an accord between the citizens of Europe, then this implies a step forward forward towards socio-political unification, *before* the internal market.

Start with social Europe

The problem is now absolutely clear. Only two scenarios will lead to an alternative to liberal-productivism in Europe:

• either go back on the single market and return to the king of control over foreign trade which non-members such as Sweden have kept;
• or accelerate, before the completion of the single market, the social and political unification of Europe in a progressive direction – measures such as Europe-wide minimum wage and working hours, common financing of social security in line with the highest level, and ecological provisions.

The first solution is in no way incompatible with increased technical and scientific cooperation, as exemplified by *ESPRIT, COMET, Ariane, Airbus* and the like. It allows each country once more to apply the compensating mechanisms of the golden age of the Common Market – freedom to determine internal compromises in fiscal and social matters, and control over its own currency. In this way Sweden, a country with high exports and highly competitive in the most sophisticated fields, regularly devalues its currency – the last time by 18 per cent. This does not increase market share (with full employment they have no need) but with exported goods bringing in more Swedish krona, it is easier to lubricate the social wheels and finance ecological choices.

This scenario is undoubtedly less beneficial than the second one. It is better to have a Europe which is progressive (in the alternative sense of the word) than a France, a Sweden etc. which are progressive in isolation. Applying the alternative in a single country is second best to applying it in Europe as a whole. Union is strength, and, as they say, the more the merrier. However, the *present* dilemma does not lie here. We are asked to choose between a Europe of *possibly* alternative states, and a united Europe which is liberal-productivist. My response is that if this is the choice, the first solution is better; but if it is possible to opt for the second scenario (a social and ecological Europe *before* a market Europe), then this must be considered.

A variant of the second scenario was suggested by François Mitterrand in his 1988 presidential campaign, and can be summarized thus: 'Let us establish a market Europe; it will be so intolerable that we will have to superimpose on it a social Europe.' With respect, I have my doubts. A liberal-productivist Europe is just as possible as the United States or Brazil. It would be a two-speed Europe in social matters, with rich and poor regions, and poor people (Turks, north Africans . . . or women) in the rich regions to serve the rich, who would all consume goods produced in the poor regions, such as the Douro region in Portugal. The single market without a social Europe is the royal gateway to this scenario of the unacceptable.

However, let us look at the problems of the second scenario – that of ecological and social Europe. Social and political unification means primarily that member countries do not conduct a trade war using 'competitive austerity', that they stop basing their growth on the slow German rate.[7] It also means that there are net transfers from richer countries to poorer countries. This of course exists in European regional programmes (which fortunately were stepped up at the Bonn summit) and the Common Agricultural Policy . . . which is not in good health.

It is normal for clever journalists, inspired by a kind of 'anti-peasant racism', to mock the never-ending discussions on the CAP. They are wrong to do this, since the CAP is the epitome of international social solidarity, with net transfers between countries. But the system is flawed in being based on income support through product prices. This tends to overproduction, subsidizing of 'farm factories' regardless of standards of care, and saturation of land and water by pesticides and imported fertilizer creating highly vulnerable 'bacterial deserts', polluting water tables and driving away poverty-stricken small farmers. The Community response, encouraged by Jacques Delors and Michel Rocard, was to keep the system but restrict production by quotas and set-aside – in other words, concentrate subsidized productivism on a limited number of small farmers and 'set aside' people and their land. Can this really be an intelligent thing to do?

These journalists make no mention of a choice of society, of culture, of health, of countryside, of beauty; merely derision directed at summit talks on the price of lupins. But these are just as important as the Matignon agreement of 1936 or the Grenelle agreement of 1968, as an institutional compromise between social groups *in several countries* to establish who gets what. In the social Europe accompanying the single market, there will be annual negotiations of this kind to establish whether retired people in Portugal with no contributions should have the same pension as retired people in Denmark, and whether British engineers, Belgian dentists or Italian entrepreneurs should pay for it. There will be, as in France in the 1950s, 'zone reductions' (that is, permitted differences between regions) affecting collective agreements and the European minimum wage. It may be far from simple, but it is what 'building Europe', politically and socially, is all about.

What would an alternative Common Agricultural Policy be like? The one proposed by the European left-wing small farmers' unions (in France, the *Confédération paysanne*) would make an audit of European land potential and the needs of its inhabitants. It would gradually move away from import patterns which have devastated the Third World because huge crops of soya and oil-seed have replaced staple food crops. A heavy tax on soya imports would finance a fund to re-establish Third World self-sufficiency in food. It would reinstate natural feeding processes for cattle, and end intensive poultry and pig rearing before villages are buried in slurry. It would promote the most effective use of open spaces and allow small farmers to exploit the twin social utility of producing food and looking after the natural environment where townspeople can find fresh air. It would give farmers a guaranteed income, through a universal allowance or a basic minimum for their products, and would in no way subsidize excessive production.

What would be the macroeconomic policy of an alternative Europe? There would be a concerted reduction in working hours, and social welfare contributions would be organized Europe-wide to finance a social welfare programme which would be brought gradually into line with the most advantageous of the previous schemes. It would issue credit money to finance transfers to the poorer regions, and to boost investment in infrastructure and education. It would protect its non-productivist growth by co-development agreements with countries of the South.

Is all this realistic? In the absence of an elected European authority, the decision rests with Germany. In effect, growth in Europe as far as it concerns purchasing power and free time is severely constrained by the growth of the economy which is the most competitive, and therefore the most in surplus – that of Germany. Since the second stage of the crisis, under pressure from the Liberal Party, German governments of both left and right have gone for monetary, fiscal and social 'orthodoxy', despite a near 10 per cent unemployment rate. The riposte might be that such a 'slow but sure' growth concerns only the German nation, and is justified by its incipient demographic implosion. In fact, there was a 3–4 per cent spontaneous annual growth in per capita wealth in Germany, even without any collective growth, simply through population erosion! Because of the way EMS and the Common Market operate, German dominance allowed it to act as economics minister for the whole of Europe: by rejecting reflation at home and devaluation by its partners, it condemned them to a cycle of alternately stagnating and being in deficit to Germany. In other words, it treated the other member states as a vast market for its own goods, while at the same time not allowing them to expand their own domestic markets, thus falling into a medium-term trap.

Monetary union and redistributive mechanisms, by ending the 'external constraint' on regions in deficit, would allow this obstacle to be overcome. Nowadays, the struggle to attract capital by idiotic interest rates is the perfect counterpart of the 'competitive stagnation' referred to above, and it also leads to EEC-paralysis. Would a single central bank solve the problem? Yes, it could, but . . . how much money a year would it issue? In relation to what growth requirements? Those in Portugal, or those of the average Bavarian, childless and bloated? Obviously the only possible rule, in the absence of a central bank controlled by an elected European Parliament, would be monetary orthodoxy – create a fixed amount of new credit every year, and let people get on with it. This is how to plan for civil disturbances; and encourage the rise of various 'National Fronts' . . .

In the medium term, we can believe in a united Europe

choosing the alternative to liberal-productivism. But in the short term, it *is* somewhat unrealistic. And if we do not resign ourselves to the struggle for survival in a liberal-productivist Europe, does this mean going back to the first scenario?

There may be a third scenario which could be called, according to choice, *solidarity-based linkage* or *harmonized delinkage*. If we take as a starting point that the struggles and social compromises are still settled at the level of the old-established nations of Europe, yet bear in mind the growing willingness of Europeans to choose a future in a supra-national framework, we should go for socio-political cooperation and unification as quickly as possible, while establishing safeguards to the internal free market to allow 'local' (that is, national or regional) compromises which widespread public debate in Europe could later extend. We should not make plans for a dream Europe without the democratic means to establish itself. We should set up regulatory mechanisms to act as 'air chambers', allowing, by free decentralized experimentation, a choice of development model.

Sometimes, it is merely a matter of using existing regulators. For example, a Community-wide system of deducting VAT from exports is still the most effective way of giving free choice about how far government revenue is socialized, without distorting competition in goods. Systems of indirect taxation can be left to harmonize gradually, perhaps by sub-groups of existing countries. If national taxes on capital are incompatible with the free movement of capital, then make such taxes the main 'direct resource' of the European Community! A single currency is obviously an advantage, but if some countries want a more generous credit policy than others, then create a common 'orthodox' currency for trade with the rest of the world, and vernacular national currencies exchangeable against the Ecu at a fixed but adjustable rate. If it is impossible in present circumstances to establish a macroeconomic policy in the interests of all Europeans, then let us stop speaking of 'convergence' (towards a more restrictive policy, given the present state of the EEC) and instead organize what is divergent. Let us leave aside the countries which in adopting more radical counter-unemployment policies compromise their trade balance, since they can invoke the safeguard clauses in the Treaty of Rome. Let us make it a rule that these clauses cease to be invoked as soon as competitiveness is restored because, for example, other countries will have introduced equivalent counter-unemployment policies. Moreover, let us count on social pressure in these countries to oblige governments to introduce such policies of 'convergence'.

After all, Europe will not be made without the Europeans, by which I mean the inhabitants of Europe, wherever they come from and whatever the colour of their passport. Europe will be the work of those who have chosen to live there, be employed there, struggle and make compromises there.

The new frontier

Harmonized ecological regulations; unified capital taxation and labour norms; Europe-wide social welfare insurance; more extensive inter-regional net transfers on the trans-national European scale; maintenance of 'air chambers' between regions or nations which want to keep a particular aspect of a satisfactory social compromise – this simply means the building of a European 'grand compromise', to be negotiated between citizens residing in Europe. And this means no less than building a nation.

A nation, said the French philosopher Ernest Renan, is 'a soul, a spiritual principle. It assumes a past, yet it is resumed in the present by a tangible fact – consent and the clearly expressed desire to go on living together. The existence of a nation is a continual plebiscite.' A nation is therefore built on a grand compromise, often painful, in the name of a future which is assumed to be more radiant. Europe is the homeland of nations, and the formation of these nations spilt blood over the whole earth. They were nations usually formed in the heat of war and revolution. In Western Europe, two nation-states were established late in the day, at the end of last century – Italy and Germany, through passive revolutions, as Gramsci called them. Italy is still suffering from a lack of warmth in unifying its north and its south. And the Germany of the Second Reich and the Third Reich was later scattered into seven pieces.

It is not an easy thing to build a nation. The simplest way is a war mobilizing everybody against a common enemy, as in the conquest of a 'new frontier'. It was the conquest of the Papal States and the frontier regions of the Austro-Hungarian Empire which unified Italy, but not the Italians. Bismarck's empire was proclaimed in the Hall of Mirrors in Versailles, with Alsace-Lorraine as a wedding present. However, what the battles of Sadowa and Sedan put together was torn apart by other, savage wars.

Faced with the German Empire and a united Italy, Austria-Hungary, a constellation of nations loosely held together by the 'imperial-royal' (*kaiserlich-königlich*, or KK) administrative authority of Franz Josef, tried to acquire a common consciousness. Robert Musil, in *The Man without Qualities*,[8] gives a humorous description of the failure of a journalistic gimmick intended to give this 'Kakania' (KK-nia) the 'spiritual principle' which it lacked. A committee of sceptical bureaucrats and intellectuals gathered at the house of a genteel commoner to try to come up with a grand initiative, the 'Collateral Campaign'. Captivated by a brilliant Prussian industrialist-cum-intellectual, all they could come up with was a plan to rearm the

Austrian army with German artillery...Joseph Roth's novel *The Radetsky March*[9] tells of the collapse of this Kakania in the first few hours of the Great War. In *Die Kapuzinergruft* (The Tomb of the Capucins),[10] Roth mourned this empire, which accommodated a friendly concert of nations through a common culture and a unifying administrative system. But these factors were not enough.

Can Europe avoid the fate of another Kakania? Or will technology programmes with fancy names like *ESPRIT*, which add a bit of 'soul', merely be a 'Collateral Campaign', producing nothing more than an efficient subcontracting network for Japanese and American technology? What 'new frontier' should Europe be offered?

There is no question of bringing Europe closer together by military conquest. On the other hand, it is not absurd to contemplate the geographical but *non-military* extension of our 'little Europe', the 'liberation of our brothers' as nationalist-minded militarists would say. It may even be a moral imperative. In Eastern Europe, nations where the soul of Europe is entrenched are shaking off the yoke of totalitarianism. The liberation of the legacy of Yalta, as outlined by Emmanuel Terray,[11] can be a first 'frontier' for Europe – the extension eastwards, towards *Mitteleuropa*, of values capable of bringing Europe together.

This idea frightens the supporters of Atlanticist Europe, of liberal-productivist Europe, represented by Alain Minc's book *La grande illusion*. Extension southwards is complete, but these remain zones for subcontracting or for northern Europeans seeking the sun. Eastern Europe is different – what if Germany recovered its full force, the crucial link with the Slav world? Yet what would an Atlantic Europe be without Prague, or Warsaw, or Budapest? An over-privileged Europe, cut off from half its culture, huddled together under the protective American nuclear umbrella.

The price to pay, as Emmanuel Terray showed with

relentless logic, is a big push for peace, but this involves the whole question of European defence. What should be offered in exchange for the break-up of the Warsaw Pact, if not the dissolution of NATO? And how can this be agreed without facing the problems of a European defence? It is not for this book to discuss whether it should be classic defence, alternative defence, harrassment of an invader by guerrilla bands, non-violent civil resistance or whatever. What is crucial is that Western Europe prevents any re-closing of the (very small) window opened by the Gorbachev era. There will be no European nation if Europe merely remains a double military protectorate.

Europe cannot claim to be a liberator if it is locked into the dictatorship of liberal-productivism and the market. It can be neither a lighthouse for nations nor a hope for peace unless it is allied to the peoples of the Third World. The new geographic frontier will simply be a warlike myth if it is not based on a convergence of peace movements in East and West. United Europe will be a mere soulless hyper-market if it does not offer Europeans and humanity in general a conception of the world which everybody would want: a new way of living and working, a new internal frontier.

As the progenitor of individual freedoms and the welfare state, Europe can be the location of a new compromise between autonomy and solidarity. That is the new internal frontier – the alternative, democratic and ecological project.

Conclusion

We have now surveyed the whole cycle of problems posed by the crisis of the development model which dominated the post-war era – Fordism. Outdated technologies, inadequate productivity, 'paradoxical involvement' of workers, increasing revolt against hierarchies and the omnipotence of the state, contradictions between the internationalization of production and markets and the still-national framework of the forms of regulation – all these problems are on the agenda of the various projects competing as a way out of the last great crisis of the twentieth century. This is why, on the other side of the divide from the old Fordist paradigm, there are inevitable similarities between liberal-productivism (whose successes and impasses vie with each other in the annals of the 1980s), and the alternative project taking shape for the 1990s, which will, I hope, characterize the move into the twenty-first century. In the same way, moreover, corporatism, Stalinism and social democracy, which claimed to supply responses to the crisis of traditional liberalism, inevitably had a certain family likeness in the debates of the 1930s.

The alternative development model proposes:

- a new wages pact, based on the negotiated involvement of workers in exchange for control over the introduction of new technologies, a dynamic guarantee of employment, and an increase in free time;

• the development of the welfare state into a welfare community, with the setting up of a third sector of community work schemes which would be self-managed, contractually bound to end-users, and part of a logic of local development founded on partnership;
• a new world order based on multilateralism, with an international credit money, abolition of debt, and social clauses on free trade;
• development choices at the local level giving greater importance to the ecological optimum, and an international agency for the protection of the common domain of humanity.

In other words, the alternative labour process model is. based on the 'mobilization of the human resource'; it is not wasteful of energy or fixed capital. The macroeconomic regime of accumulation ensures full employment through the growth of free time and the third sector. The new mode of regulation is based on negotiated management by small groups and a contractualization of the relation between these groups. The new global configuration will enhance auto-centred development and agreements on co-development. As for the content of production and consumption, the aim of this will be to allow the ecological potential of the planet to be reconstituted, and its emphasis will be on cultural enrichment. A model such as this ought to bring about a change in the relationship between genders, though this is the aim of a specific struggle, not an inevitable consequence of it.

Clearly, certain practices of liberal-productivism seem to be present in this model: quality circles, part-time working, subsidized jobs, discount of international debts on the grey market . . . On questions such as these, the answers cannot be totally dissimilar.

But the overall logic of the two models is diametrically opposed. Liberal-productivism, in the form in which it seemed to triumph in the 1980s, is based on conflict involving everybody, at the local or international level. The inherent aim of this unremitting struggle is accumulation for accumulation's sake. Only the upper third of the 'hourglass society' which this creates can hope to benefit from the fruits of a 'technological revolution' reduced to an avalanche of gadgets. This upper third could find, in a diminishing middle class, allies against the tide of the dispossessed. But it would be powerless against the tide of ecological disasters which would certainly drown this unacceptable world.

At the end of the 1980s, the increase in social, macroeconomic and ecological dangers awakened a long delayed awareness. Within liberal-productivist competition are emerging more advanced social compromises, which are proving more effective.

At today's crossroads, the alternative is no longer merely desirable; it is becoming ecologically indispensible. It is proving to be socially attainable, on the basis of a new grand compromise. The alternative model would be a step forward in the conflictual reconciliation of initiative and solidarity. A step forward and no more; it would abolish neither hierarchy nor commodity relations. But it would be a step forward for future progress. Today, a small headland on our planet, choosing to unite after covering the world with the blood of its conflicts and rivalries, is hesitating over the model to adopt in common. Europe can become the test-bed of the alternative. So, let us make the bold choice! The alternative will be the new frontier of Europe.

Postscript to the English Edition

9 November 1989: the joy of liberation in Eastern Europe, the end of East–West confrontation.

27 February 1991: the horror of a war waged with a clear conscience, a war of the overwhelming superiority of advanced countries against a Third World country led by a dictator.

Between these two dates, the world was knocked off course. The twentieth century finally came to an end. The blueprint for the future, which this book originally was, became a matter of absolute urgency.

A new dawn?

On 9 November 1989, Europe became once more the focal point of history. Not, as too often in the twentieth century, to shake the world with its quarrels, covering it in blood with its conflicts, or astounding it by the enormity of its crimes; but, for once, as a symbol of peace, reconciliation and liberation. The end of the Berlin Wall meant the end of forty-five years of tensions and hatreds, of mourning and despair, of powerlessness and humiliation. The spontaneous rejoicing at the Brandenburg Gate gave a meaning, forty-five years on, to the handshakes of American and Soviet soldiers over the dead body of Nazi Germany. But the symmetry had already been broken, when crowds of East Germans, smiling or fearful, broke out to overwhelm their Western relatives with hugs and kisses. The end of the divisions of Yalta was also the complete capitulation of Stalinist state capitalism to the blandishments of the Western mix of neo-liberalism and social democracy. Not just the Cold War cycle, but the cycle started by the October Revolution, was closing on the bitter taste of widespread disarray.

This cloud of bitterness, for those who had believed in Communism, was soon thickened by sickening smells emanating from the ruins of Eastern Europe (anti-semitism, populism, unbridled materialism coming face to face with reactionary spiritualisms), and by the renewed arrogance of Kohl's Germany. However, what we must first recall is the series of celebrations which, just after the Bicentenary of the French Revolution, greeted the overthrow of 'Communist' dictatorships, from Poland to Romania. What collapsed during these glorious days was a totalitarian system in the East, and the basis of the Soviet–American condominium over Europe. We owe this double liberation primarily to the East European peoples themselves, who since 1953, in Berlin, Budapest, Warsaw and Prague, had never given up hope; to the underground activists of many decades, and to the crowds who year after year learned how to challenge the army and the militias, right up to the non-violent East German revolution of autumn 1989.

We owe it also to people in the West who in the 1980s, from Sicily to Ireland, united in their hundreds of thousands to reject Euro-missiles and the Satanization of Eastern Europe. By highlighting the crisis of the consensus on NATO nuclear defence, and in showing Soviet leaders that, because there were pacifists in the West as well as the East, the Soviet Union no longer needed an expensive buffer zone, West European peace movements did infinitely more for the liberation of their East European brothers than the thousands of megatons in Polaris submarines, or on the

Plateau d'Albion in southern France.

This must be the first conclusion to be drawn from what has happened: the final condemnation of nuclear blackmail, of the ignoble slogan of supporters of nuclear deterrence 'Better dead than red.' The Polish people were right not to commit suicide in 1981. The emergence from 'totalitarianism' was just as difficult, but just as certain, as the end of Franco- or Pinochet-style 'authoritarianism'. The struggle for freedom will never be based on the annihilation of humanity. The modernization of nuclear weapons is henceforth unjustifiable. The French defence budget in particular should immediately have been frozen, and the money directed to more pressing needs, while defence policies were being reviewed.

It is, after all, the whole global geo-strategic framework which has been recast. East–West polarization is a thing of the past, surviving only because of limited imagination. All the institutions of the Cold War – NATO and the Warsaw Pact – as well as the European Community, need to be looked at again. This is the major focus of the 1990s, after the shake-up of 1989.

When the Berlin Wall was breached, I was in a small town in Greece, at a study group on a progressive approach to North–South relations, attended each year by intellectuals, politicians and leaders of non-governmental organizations from Europe and the Third World. The Africans there noted with amusement how shattered the Europeans were. For them, it showed that their dictatorships and single parties propped up by West European governments, such as Houphouët-Boigny in the Ivory Coast and Mobutu in Zaire, would also disappear one day. But the Yugoslav member did not hide his anxiety, warning that the German right was planning a Fourth Reich, and already trying to recover Slovenia. Hope and anxiety: Berlin has again become the umbilical cord of Europe.

The economic consequences of the end of the Cold War

The consequences of the current upheavals are in fact impossible to calculate, even just in the economic field. We are reminded of the youthful Keynes writing his first major work after the First World War, *The Economic Consequences of the Peace*. Nobody today is as talented as he was, and the problems are infinitely more complex. Let us, however, at least try to put the problems.

Applying literally the title of Keynes's book, the speeding up of the arms race played an important part in the 1980s. It ruined the Soviet Union and the United States, while providing a stable and predictable market for high-tech industries. This was the cause of the American 'double deficit' – in its budget and its trade balance. The deficit created a natural outlet for Europe and the 'Japanese co-prosperity sphere'; and it caused no trade balance problems, as a domestic boom would have done. American debt, however, pushed up interest rates and, together with Third World debt, threatened world financial stability.

There is no longer any reason for the arms race today. Thousands of billions of dollars are potentially available to boost welfare growth, settle debts and fight against the world ecological crisis. France, for example, would have huge fiscal reserves to finance the renewal of its education system and its research. But let us not get carried away. Geo-strategic conservatism is still powerful. It has the support of military-industrial lobbies stressing the loss of jobs by cutting military levels, and overestimating the difficulties of a planned reconversion of the arms industry; it is also fed by (or even provokes) new tensions arising from the break-up of the Soviet empire. This is what the Gulf War and tensions in Eastern Europe have shown. After all, the disappearance of one kind of tension does not eliminate all tensions; the end of a nightmare does not prevent death spasms. In the disoriented Europe which is groping for a new order, ethnic tensions and national ambitions will again be centre stage.

Ethnic tensions mean a grave danger that the economic crisis in Eastern Europe cannot be solved, including that in countries such as Poland and Hungary, which might have chosen the path of liberal-productivism. Already, after initial democratic euphoria, the old demons of authoritarian populism are again rearing their heads, in alliances (unthinkable yesterday, but so logical tomorrow) between bureaucratic conservatisms and national, even religious, chauvinisms – an alliance between the right wings of the Communist apparatus and former opposition groups. The danger is that new powerful states will assert themselves in this way, and direct hostility on to 'outsiders' – Romanians against Hungarians, Balts against Russians, Serbs against Croats, and everybody against resilient Jews. The fading of the nuclear apocalypse will begin a new age of 'small wars' against a background of suffering, such as are endemic in Northern Ireland or the Spanish Basque country.

National ambitions lead one to think of a Germany of 80 million people. From economic giant and political pygmy, Germany has suddenly become economic superpower and political giant. In recent times, its strength was threatened by demographic decline. Suddenly, it could contemplate gathering under its wing not only East Germany, but also Austria, no longer ruled out by its neutrality, and all remaining ethnic Germans from the other side of the former Iron Curtain, providing markets and skilled or cheap workers beyond its needs.

The new German Question

We can see here the lack of perception of those French writers of the 1980s who, raising fears of German hegemony, rejected an enlarged neutralist Europe in favour of an Atlanticist one. From now on, this fear can be dissipated only by the counterbalance of a Europe stretching beyond Germany to the small nations of *Mitteleuropa*. Beginning in autumn 1989, meetings between Italy, Yugoslavia, Austria, Hungary and Czechoslovakia heralded the return of the pre-war 'Little Entente' between nations springing from the break-up of the Austro-Hungarian Empire, the ancient barrier to the ambitions of Prussian Germany.

It is true that in 1989 Germany struck fear into people's hearts. In Poland, Solidarity called on the Red Army for protection; France found a certain attraction in Margaret Thatcher. At that level, a subjective feeling becomes an objective fact. The underlying causes of this need to be understood.

It is not enough to be frightened of a unified Germany. What is crucial is to understand why West Germany was so strong on its own. Although 1989 saw the final victory of Western market capitalism over Eastern state capitalism, forty-five years after their joint defeat of Nazism, there was also a more subtle victory – by one kind of market capitalism over another. Ten years after the ultra-liberal offensive in the former masters of the world (the United States and Britain), the debate over the share-out of the spoils of 'socialism in being' reveal one crucial fact: these two countries plus France, despite their nuclear weapons, have no contribution to make because they are weak and debt-ridden. The new division of the world is between the poles of Japan and Germany.

With 65 million people, West Germany had half the population of Japan. In 1989, its exports were worth $382 billion, giving a trade surplus of $81 billion, compared with Japan's $77 billion. This was achieved, as everyone knows, with a standard of living for wage-earners which is incomparably higher, and without any particular specialization in new technologies. Germany comes off best without electronic chips, and with a labour force among the most expensive in the world!

What Japan and West Germany realized first and foremost (and before them Volvo in Sweden, at its Kalmar plant) was that workers need to be involved in the productivity learning process, in the search for quality, and in the management of production flows. 'Kanban' was superior to 'material requirement planning' because 'negotiated involvement' was superior to neo-liberal 'flexibility'.[1] And behind this was the victory not only of a particular conception of unionism, but of the intelligence of a certain kind of employer. Germany's superiority lay in the fact that the 'Kalmarian' capital–labour compromise was more widespread there than in Japan.

German superiority is based on a wide network of collective sector agreements, drawn up at regional level, then decentralized down to co-management committees. As in the United States, German unions in the 1970s at first resisted, to protect jobs. But in the 1980s, with unemployment at 10 per cent, they mounted a counter-offensive: subjective involvement by workers in return for shorter hours. This was an approach with a long pedigree – in 1925, the DGB (German Labour Union Confederation) was already saying that 'high wages, short hours, rational methods of production and rational organization of the economy are the prerequisites of German economic progress and competitiveness'.

This industrial sector unionism has extracted the promise of a 35-hour week from 1995, but it has certain drawbacks: it excludes 'poor' sectors such as services, and it favours a dualism to the detriment of women, Turks and future 'brothers from the East', just as '*Untermenschen*' were excluded in the past. The Swedish union movement has gone this stage further, and extends its protection to all sectors of society (at the risk of 'overheating').[2]

Germany is not an alternative model, and Japan even less so, even though Germany is socially more 'advanced'. These countries have shown the productive *possibility* of development models based on negotiated involvement. Everything will depend on the level of *solidarity* towards which social pressure will lead them. For without solidarity, of course, negotiated involvement leads to a *wage-earning aristocracy* sustaining a new imperialism.

It is for this reason that there is a new fear of Germany, just as in Asia there is a fear of Japan. It is not that the Germans have a Nazi chromosome in their make-up. They are simply rich and powerful, like the United States. Germany needs to be feared as Mexico and Canada fear the United States – no more and no less. Except on one point! The United States does not lay claim to Lower California or British Colombia. Helmut Kohl, however, to gain extreme-right support, refused for some months to recognize the Oder-Neisse line as the Polish-German frontier, and became the most unpopular man in Europe. Brandt's Germany was a beacon for Eastern Europe; Kohl's Germany was a nightmare. It is not that Kohl was like Hitler, but that he was like Reagan, ignoring his West European partners, humiliating his East European clients, and sacrificing the external image of his country to the demagogic manipulation of support from the most re-actionary part of his electorate.

The way in which he imposed German unification is significant. In December 1989, the democratic revolution in East Germany was still hoping to recreate the Eastern *Länder* on a different model from Western materialism. The hesitations of the Communist Prime Minister Mödrow disheartened the East Germans, and they resigned them-selves to unity at any price, which is their right. However, Kohl added fuel to the flames by saying 'Stay where you are and I'll buy you out. In the meantime, don't do any-thing excessive!'. If this was the case, they might as well emigrate immediately. Moreover, monetary unification changed nothing. The sudden linking of such divergent price systems and levels of productivity raised tensions even more, ruined thousands of industrial concerns in the East and sent the unemployed fleeing westwards.

When the United States under Truman helped the economic recovery of Europe and Japan, it set up 'air locks' consisting of a right to protectionism, currency non-convertibility, and gifts and loans under the Marshall Plan. Kohl did the exact opposite – no help for economic recovery, but scooping up the remnants.

This absurd situation cannot last. The eastern part of Germany will have to be rebuilt as it stands, with living standards and investment financed from the West. Germany can find the money either by raising taxes in the West (on capital, for example, which is taxed at a very low rate), though Kohl's voters would not like this, or by issuing money at low interest rates, which would fuel inflation, and the Bundesbank would not like that. In effect, Kohl bought out East Germany without putting money up front, like a Wall Street raider with junk bonds. Since everyone can see that it has to be paid for at some time in the future, interest rates will go on rising to the detriment of the whole of Europe, from Italian investors to young French couples.

This is the German problem. The Single Act unified the European economy, but no provision was made for European democratic unification. Because of this, economic policy and the daily life of Europeans is determined in the dominant state – Germany. It is not the fault of a people who wanted to be unified; it is primarily the fault of those who wanted to build Europe exclusively through the power of money.

The premature crisis of the European Community

Beyond this, it is the very structure of Western Europe which is challenged by any move towards a 'Big Europe' including 'Middle Europe'; that is, all of Eastern Europe except the former Soviet Union. The break-up of the Soviet empire happened in 1991, though it is unlikely that its peoples, except for the Balts, could join Europe in the foreseeable future. However, the predictable crisis of the European Community became clear throughout 1989, quite independently of events in the East.

This book has made the point that the project for a large single market in 1993 contained a major contradiction. A single market for capital and goods without common fiscal, social and ecological policies could not fail to set off a downward competition between member states, each needing to bring its trade into balance. To deal with the threat of 'social dumping', Jacques Delors counted on a push *after the event* by unions in peripheral and social democratic countries to impose common statutory or contractual bases throughout the Community.

This has not happened, despite the (half-hearted) protestations of the European Parliament. We have seen in this book how attempts to harmonize VAT failed; how France saw to it that there are still customs barriers in Europe after 1992. However, lack of harmonization on capital taxation is much more serious. To provide for the free movement of capital from July 1990, the European Commission proposed in February 1989 a 15 per cent levy at source on investment income. Not much, but better than nothing. On 1 June 1989, Germany abolished its own tax! The result was, to quote Michel Charasse, the French budget minister, that 'France reacted by slightly reducing its withholding taxes on saving.' In effect, in France after 1 January 1990, income from open-end investment companies are free of tax up to 25,000 frs. a month, more than most wage-earners receive! We are therefore moving towards a Europe where only wage-earners and consumers will be taxed . . .

Even more serious was the surrender over social Europe.

In September 1989, the European Commission proposed an insipid Social Charter. On 22 November 1989, the European Parliament, the only representative body of European peoples, voted for 'a minimum base below which the Council would not go'.[3] This was a synthesis of everything that wage-earners had achieved in Europe, including the right to a minimum wage, 'the gradual harmonization of social welfare benefits at the highest level', the participation of workers in technological decisions and in the organization of work . . . However, in December 1989, the European summit leaders (apart from Thatcher) adopted the Commission's Charter, even further diluted – and the press did not even publish it! The Parliament, which had stated that if this zero-charter were adopted it would block the single market, did not react. The 39 Green members prepared a motion of censure against the Commission, which could have been passed if the left - Social Democrats and Communists – had voted for it. But the plan came to nothing.

In December 1991, at Maastricht, the twelve governments of the European Community agreed on how political Europe would be structured. However, the Maastricht agreement did not address itself to the real problems. There was no serious move towards democratic control by elected Parliaments. On the contrary, Maastricht gave rise to a legal monstrosity – legislative power in Europe was handed over to coordination by national governments, a state apparatus on auto-pilot. Social Europe was of course once more sacrificed, and reduced to a 'zero Charter', with Britain opting out. The final point is that areas vital for an ecologically sustainable development were not included in the agreement. In a referendum in June 1992, Denmark, the 'good boy of Europe', the most advanced in social and ecological terms, rejected the Maastricht agreement.

In essence, as it is at present emerging, Europe will be unified only for the sake of capital, to allow it to escape from state control; that is, from the tax authorities and from social legislation. We cannot say that this Europe is 'apolitical'. It has a policy – that of Bonn, with a few concessions. And it may be that the Monetary Union will confer all power in monetary matters on the Bundesbank. What this Europe lacks is the democratic control which alone would allow the interests of the vast majority of Europeans to be represented, and therefore the Community desired by Europe to coalesce round a grand compromise. Today, only 'social matters' mould community consciousness, as was seen in the debate on German unification.

The danger of a two-speed Europe in social matters has become great, with the rich regions of northern Europe keeping advanced Kalmarian-type social compromises (negotiated involvement, high wages) thanks to their technological supremacy, and 'neo-Taylorist' ordinary industries with temporary and low-paid workforces migrating to the periphery – the British Isles or the Iberian peninsula.[4]

Four circles of expansion

The arrival of Eastern Europe on the scene upset this scheme of things, positively and negatively. A positive effect was that West Germany, by absorbing East Germany, became a young nation with significant reconstruction needs. It is bound to become once more a driving force for the rest of Europe – even France, Britain and Portugal will pick up new markets in the old East Germany. In the medium term, the question is much more complex, and everything will depend on the new structure for Europe. What circles were already there round Europe?

First, there is the European Free Trade Area – Switzerland, Austria and Scandinavia. These countries were as wealthy and socially advanced as the Federal Republic, if not more so, and they refused to join the EEC in order to safeguard their neutrality and their internal compromises, which were inspired more by 'Kalmarism' than by liberal-productivism. They already have free access to the EEC, but fear the protectionism of the post-1993 single market. With the disappearance of the military dimension, they will be tempted to force an entry into the EEC, which would strengthen the hand of those who favour a social Europe.

The second circle is formed by the southern rim of the Mediterranean – the semi-developed countries of the Preferential Interest Agreement, from Morocco to Turkey. Already hurt by privileged access to northern European markets on the part of the periphery countries of the EEC (Spain, Portugal, Greece), they are trying to become more closely associated with the Community, and would be the big losers from an incursion by Eastern Europe, which is ethnically more 'acceptable'. These Mediterranean countries are in an often terrifying economic and ecological crisis (in Algeria and Egypt), made worse by demographic explosion. The irresistible upsurge of Muslim fundamentalism in these countries is a sign of the failure of Western-style productivist and statist models. The European Commission, conscious of this 'time bomb', proposed a doubling of EEC financial aid to these countries, bringing it to 50 p per EEC citizen per year, and £2 for every person in receipt of this aid. This is a derisory sum indicating the emergence of a new 'hostile frontier' on the southern flank of Europe; we will come back to this later.

Then, beyond the seas and south of the Sahel, there are the African-Caribbean-Pacific countries. The renewal in December 1989 of the Lomé Agreement between them and the European Community was a tremendous disappointment. The EEC, in being mean with economic support to these countries, chose not to be the driving force of world development. This is worrying . . . for Eastern Europe.

It is these Eastern European countries which form the fourth circle, divided into three categories. With a per capita gross product equal to that of Spain ($7,800), the former East Germany ($7,200) and Czechoslovakia ($6,000) have only their bureaucratic chaos, lack of internal consensus, and isolation to blame for the fact that they have wasted their pre-war industrial and cultural heritage, but they could easily catch up again. The second group, however, are on a par with Algeria and South Korea ($2,500 per capita per year) – Hungary, Yugoslavia ($2,300) and Poland ($1,900 per capita, ten times less than the former Federal Republic). Moreover, these countries are burdened with debt (respectively $20, $23, and $39 billion) and crippled by inflation. In the third group are Bulgaria, Romania, most of the former Yugoslavia and Albania. In many economic and cultural aspects, these countries are close to the second circle of non-EEC countries. They are a kind of greater 'Turkey in Europe', and in fact they were once part of the Turkish Empire (as was Greece, though it is now of course an EEC member).

The scenario of the unacceptable

Faced with this European Third World appearing in the East, moderate social democrats in the EEC, particularly Jacques Delors and François Mitterrand, saw the danger – that the trap of the Single Act was being sprung for them. They had set up a Europe of traders and capital, thinking that the rest would follow as Europe unified politically; but now there appeared the spectre of an enlarged free-trade zone amenable to no supra-national social regulation. So they tried to force matters by consolidating the Europe of the Twelve and collectively managing relations with the

East. Unfortunately they threw away their trump cards by signing the Single Act in 1985, and Kohl's Germany won the game. The Maastricht agreement improved nothing.

The opposite position was that of financial circles and neo-liberal politicians, led by Thatcher. They wanted to extend to Eastern Europe free-trade relations under firm control, of the Preferential Interest Agreement kind, and block attempts by the Delors Commission to move to a social Europe. The implacable mechanism of a multi-speed Europe in social matters would then apply to Eastern Europe as well, leaving Africa and even Ireland, Portugal and Greece to their sad fate. Under the pressure of debt, and at the cost of a few billion dollars of emergency aid, a huge free zone of low wage and virtually non-unionized subcontracting would open up in the East, for labour-intensive industries to serve the financial and technical centres of north-west Europe.

The strength of this scenario is that it offers Germany the royal road of à la carte satellization of central Europe. In return for five years of economic liberalization, West Germany acting with Austria could absorb the markets and skilled labour of East Germany, solving its demographic problem for a generation. Czechoslovakia and the northern ex-Yugoslav republic of Slovenia could play the role of Spain outside the EEC, with heavy industry and engineering. Hungary, Poland (with governments which are already ultra-liberal) and the rest of Yugoslavia would become, in the style of Tunisia or Morocco, devoted to textiles, neo-Taylorist assembly industries and growing potatoes . . . but in return for import quotas – subcontracting yes, invasion no. This economic 'Fourth Reich', resembling the Japanese sphere, would no doubt on its outer fringes be prey to nationalist 'small wars', such as those in Northern Ireland or the Spanish Basque country, and even a 'serious war' as in Yugoslavia. It is a scenario which is not very attractive, but initially it is economically dynamic. And it is the most likely one.

This scenario, the most likely one, is unacceptable. Not only would it hasten the split within Western Europe between 'Kalmarian' regions and 'neo-Taylorist' ones, but it would set the latter in direct competition with the 'second circle' – the countries of the southern rim of the Mediterranean. It would no longer be a matter of subsidizing their standard of living, and their membership of the European Community would be in doubt. Within Europe, there would be a new frontier – that of poverty, of the mafia, of Third-Worlding. This frontier would no longer be the Mediterranean and the Iron Curtain. It would exclude the Iberian peninsula (except Catalonia), perhaps Corsica, certainly Sicily and Italy south of Rome; it would include Slovenia but not Kosovo, Transylvania but not Moldavia, the Baltic republics but certainly not the Soviet Muslim republics. In short, 'legitimate Europe' would have the frontier which it once had with the Arab and Turkish empires.

This new apartheid would clearly be based on racism directed against a Muslim world embracing fundamentalism; a world which could without difficulty be accused of violating human rights and especially women's rights, and rejected as 'barbarian'.[5] But there would also be racism within Europe – rich regions against poor ones, West Germans against their 'Eastern brothers' and all Slavs, northern Italians against southern Italians, and so on.

North-west Europe would become more than ever a rich people's club, barricaded against demographic and religious threat from the South. To economic imperialism and cultural contempt could well be added 'eco-imperialism', whereby north-west Europe would reject polluting industries not by questioning its own overconsumption but by sending them to its southern frontier.

The new frontier, again

A third scenario is possible – hold up the free-market parts of the Single Act until there is a parallel ecological and social section in place; and make Eastern Europe, associated with the EEC in ways already tried and tested for southern Europe, into a kind of test-bed for a move towards a confederate Europe – an ecological and social Europe, but made up of nations or regions with a certain socio-cultural autonomy. This would mean massive aid, and writing off debt by a reform of the international financial system to include the Third World, as this book proposes. This grand confederal Europe would reduce the danger of German hegemony and 'small wars'.

It may be a dream scenario, but there are hopeful signs: pressure within the EEC from unions, social movements and most MEPs for an ecological and social Europe in solidarity with other peoples; resistance by East Germans to the dismantling of their welfare state; the emergence of a civil society in Poland and Hungary with reservations about IMF 'recipes' and the free-market approach of their governments; solid and flourishing markets in the East to offset any instability in the countries of the former Soviet Union. In the course of history, reason sometimes wins out. This is called progress.

A different Europe is possible – ecological, social and democratic in its overall decisions, but regionally diverse in its life-styles; taming blind market forces through a common base of social rights and ecological duties; mobilizing its financial and technical resources to make standards of living equal in different regions. This can be the ideological cement and the mobilizing vision of European unification in the conquest of a new frontier – a new frontier in the East, and especially a new internal frontier. A new frontier of solidarity with the Third World.

This was (and still is) the project of European Greens and a section of the 'Euro-left', which together mobilized against the second Gulf War.

The world after the Gulf War

On 28 February 1991 the second Gulf War ended, and the masks slipped.

Men and women of good faith who until January 1991 had believed in a just war, and who even after 15 January were in favour to a war for the liberation of Kuwait and for democracy, had to accept, their eyes opened by the 'slaughter of the innocents' of 15–23 February when Iraq tried in vain to surrender, that what was happening was nothing less than the destruction of a state and the crushing of a people. The pretext, of course, was an excellent one – Saddam Hussein's crazy aggression, his crass obstinacy, his threat of further crimes, even if not carried out . . . But as soon as the criminal looked as if he was surrendering, the dispensers of justice, reluctant to lose a single minute's bombing, cried 'Wait! There are still a few bridges standing, factories working, water supplies intact!'.

Even more shameful, if that is possible, was the peace (or is it already the third Gulf War?). As soon as the Al-Sabah dynasty returned to Kuwait, it tried to re-establish its hereditary dictatorship, ignoring the democratic forces of the Kuwaiti resistance. The approach adopted to the insurrection in northern and southern Iraq by the Forces of Righteousness, to the disgust of their own officers (their commander George Bush had just called on the Iraqi people to rise up against Saddam), was that of Bismarck to the Paris Commune of 1870–1: give the defeated regime the means for the bloody suppression of popular insurrection. Violating a ceasefire which had only just been signed, Saddam's helicopters took off again to asphyxiate Kurds and Shiites, as they had done three years earlier. The Allies were faced with an outcry from Western public opinion horrified by this kind of realpolitik, that of millions of Kurdish refugees hounded by this 'new Hitler', set up again by Bush as the butcher of the Iraqi people; and the Allies resigned themselves to a very belated humanitarian operation . . . but only after the Kurds had been 'Palestinized'. Powerful nations like peoples only when they are down, especially if their suffering is photogenic.[6]

A new world is rising from the ruins of Iraq, unlike the one which the fall of the Berlin Wall promised. It is a world once more divided into two, but this time between the North (together with its honourable correspondents in the palaces of the South) and the South (together with its ambassadors in the suburbs of the North).

The case of Saddam

It must be said that at the beginning everything went well. The condemnation of Iraq, after so many of its crimes had gone unpunished, was for the first time accompanied by immediate sanctions. At last, the United Nations was becoming both the architect and the enforcer of a world of law. There was not too much concern over this confusion of judicial and executive functions – wrongly, since by ignoring the International Court at The Hague, a choice had already been made not to go for a solution based on law. Very quickly there came a barrage of protests: these 'dispensers of justice' had covered up the Iraqi Baathists' crimes (aggression against Iran in 1980, gassing the Kurds in 1988) and ignored many equivalent ones. But they were silenced: 'We have to begin somewhere, so let's start with Saddam, and then see about the others.'

Was this approach credible? After the liberation of Kuwait, would sanctions be imposed to force Israel to obey

UN resolutions, Turkey to evacuate Cyprus, Syria to leave Lebanon? These can merely be guesses. It is true that there were never such categorical statements from governments as after this war: 'This time we must do something to help the Palestinians, assist Lebanon, tackle the Cyprus problem.'[7] It seems that a debt has been contracted to the Idea of Law. Will it be honoured? I sincerely hope so, but it is not just the past (before the 2 August 1990 Iraqi invasion of Kuwait) or the present (the Kurdish problem) that worries me. As I see it, the setting up of the anti-Saddam alliance, *after* 2 August and not before, is as bad a sign for the future as the more distant past. After all, it was *after* 2 August and Resolution 660 that President Mubarak took Egyptian democracy a giant step backwards; after 2 August that Syrian control over Lebanon was acknowledged; after the Al-Aqsa massacre (8 October) that Israel ignored a further Security Council resolution; on 6 November that Saudi Arabia, host to a UN army, cynically breached the Universal Declaration of Human Rights by suppressing a demonstration of women trying to assert their rights; on 14 January that the Soviets intervened in Lithuania; on 15 January, before any Scud attack, that Israel imposed a precautionary curfew on a permanent basis in the Occupied Territories.

How could the defenders of the Just Crusade forget that the basic characteristic of law is universality? That a law applying only to rich Kuwaitis, and ignored in the case of Palestinians in their ghetto, not only does not deserve to be called a law, but makes the whole idea of law absurd?

The basic truth about the Gulf War was immediately apparent for anybody able to read – no more and no less than the destruction and dismantling of Iraq as a country. If the aim had been merely to free Kuwait, sanctions would have been enough. Did the South Africans have less to lose by ending apartheid than Saddam by giving up a Kuwait rendered valueless by those very sanctions? Even the leaky sanctions against South Africa had a decisive effect after four years. The problem with sanctions against Iraq was that they were likely to be effective more quickly – the 'catastrophe scenario' fully admitted in February 1991 (as opposed to the hesitations after August 1990) was that Saddam would leave Kuwait with his military-industrial complex intact.

Here is a real problem which opponents of the war (and those who therefore supported sanctions – we can call them pacifists) did not highlight enough. Iraqi military power, to which all coalition countries, including the former Soviet Union, had contributed during the Iran–Iraq war, together with the imperialist stance of the Iraqi Baathists, constituted a permanent threat to the region. Sanctions should have been extended (by a specific resolution) to the non-conventional disarming of Iraq, to a redirection of its conventional weapons. Let us not forget that it was 'pacifists' who (to the deafening silence of the media) had for ten years denounced the sale of arms to an Iraq which had attacked Iran.

Why then did the West turn against its former ally? The reasons are the usual ones – first, to rub out the traces of collusion. There is something of the 'killing of Frankenstein's monster' in what happened, to which the Noriega case can be seen as a dress rehearsal. Nasser always maintained that Saddam Hussein was another CIA agent. In any event, he loyally served the West's interests until the West grew alarmed at the growing autonomy of the little monster. He had to be destroyed, by exploiting his first mistake, or even setting a trap for him.[8]

However, like Noriega, this former ally immediately managed to gather round him the latent hatred of the masses against 'Zionism and the Americans'. In all Arab countries where for some time there had been the beginnings of democracy (Algeria, Tunisia, Jordan, Yemen), mobilization by the people determined the position of

the government. Only dictatorships, with two excep-
tions (Mauritania and Sudan), supported the coalition.
Anti-coalition feeling even gave Moroccan public opinion
a chance of emancipation in opposition to Hassan II.
This was to be expected, despite deliberate blindness on
the part of intellectuals on the side clamouring for war.
However, this hatred *could* have been forestalled. All it
needed was a solemn Security Council undertaking to solve
concomitantly the Palestinian problem on the basis of
Resolution 242. But this would have been 'giving a ransom
to the aggressor'! This is a strange argument, in that 242
predated 660 by a mere quarter of a century. Instead they
went for the usual tactic – to deal with the 'creature of
Frankenstein' (yesterday Iran, today Iraq), assemble a
coalition of creatures who are just as respectable (from
Fahd to Assad), and prepare for a third Gulf War.

Why this apparently absurd choice? Because the revival
of Arabic and Islamic nationalism under Saddam was a
much greater danger than the Baathist regime on its own.
Behind the regime was the growing menace of the Iraqi
nation-state – the only country in the Middle East which
was more or less viable, since it had oil, water and a large
population; and it was aiming at nuclear capability in an
Arab world which itself was a prey to Islamic fervour – the
latest challenge to Western arrogance after the collapse of
Communism.[9]

The destruction of Iraq was therefore the primary aim of
the war – Iraq as a *country*, and not as a Baathist regime or
even Saddam Hussein's power base, and certainly not as a
buffer state such as the British had set up. Of course,
George Bush wanted a successor to emerge from within
the dictatorship who was more presentable and more
submissive. Yet the choice between keeping Saddam
and having a revolution by an Iraqi opposition of Kurds,
Islamic fundamentalists and Communists was an easy one –
Saddam became less of a problem.

After the 17 January 1991 attack, the inhabitants of Baghdad were without water and electricity. Overall, the equivalent of half a dozen Hiroshima bombs were dropped on Iraq. Even after the evacuation of Kuwait, any reconstruction remained impossible. The people of Iraq, set back in time by several decades, wallowed in polluted puddles among ruined buildings, under the threat of famine and epidemics.

The cost of this victory, by which a people was torn apart, is clear: the hatred of a whole region, Western values discredited, the probable triumph of Islamic fundamentalism in several countries. It is very likely that this cost was taken on board by the decision makers; but it is greater than the advantage gained from the destruction of Iraq. What was decided in high places was that *in any case* tensions between North and South were bound to increase, and that higher interests were at stake, which prescribed the immediate use of a policy of strength. We must look at these higher interests, and discuss the two 'real motives' usually quoted to explain the shambles.

First, however, a methodological word of warning – wars cannot be explained by their end-results, even though these were the aims (acknowledged or not) in the minds of decision makers. The dynamic of the 'road to war' involves many determinants – psychological and even psychoanalytical. This is very clear in the case of the loser, but also in the case of the victors. Bush's 'macho' anti-Saddam speeches show the need to wipe out the humiliation of Vietnam, hardly achieved by the ridiculous operations in Grenada and Panama. This need to 'show you've got what it takes' was probably vital in gaining the eventual support (it was not clear at the beginning) of public opinion. The 'basic interests' which will now be analysed were vital in obtaining the support of 'reasonable people'. The word is 'interests' and not 'causes' – we are looking at the *expected results* of the war, which were more and more clearly perceived during the lead-up to war, and not at the 'immediate causes', such as the invasion of Kuwait and the American desire for revenge.

A war for oil?

This was an analysis which was widespread among pacifists, but also generally accepted by public opinion, and sometimes cynically admitted by Western leaders, from George Bush to Michel Rocard, or even by intellectuals in the warmonger camp. It is obviously an analysis which is largely justified, but it needs significant qualification and refinement.

We can dismiss straightaway the crude version of this line of reasoning, whereby *in the short term* (that is, after 2 August 1990), Iraq had to be prevented from dominating the oil market. As early as autumn 1990, Zbigniew Brzezinski, a former Carter advisor, was saying that enough replacement oil could be sent quickly from Saudi Arabia, and it was not even necessary to liberate Kuwait.[10] The figures prove this: Iraq represents 4.5 per cent of the world output of crude oil, and Saudi Arabia 12 per cent.[11] Overrunning Kuwait gave Iraq an extra 3 per cent. How ludicrous to die for 3 per cent!

Of course, the matter becomes more serious when the Kuwaiti 3 per cent is considered as part of the *exportable* volume available to the world market, and particularly to the armoury of the main body regulating this market – OPEC, with 36.9 per cent of world output. It must not be forgotten that the world's main producer, the former USSR with 19.5 per cent, is less and less able to export, and the second largest producer, the United States with 13.7 per cent, already imports nearly half of its oil requirements.

Within OPEC there have been two conflicting approaches since 1973. On one side are countries with a small population whose needs are already met, which are trying to maximize and spin out their oil revenues. Their strategy is to prevent excessive prices (higher than $15 a barrel) forcing consumer countries into energy saving or energy substitution. The Gulf 'oil kingdom' bloc, with a good third of OPEC production, champions this approach. On the other side are populous countries which try to maximize short-term profit in order to reinvest (soundly or otherwise – industrialization or arms). Algeria, Iran and Iraq (nearly a third of OPEC production) represent this second approach and aim at a price of around $25 a barrel. The two groups were at loggerheads at the July 1990 OPEC Conference, where Iraq won a $21 target price, and Kuwait increased its output to bring prices down. This conflict was one of the precursors of the war and doubtless the direct cause of the Iraqi invasion.

The effect of the annexation of Kuwait was to shift about 10 per cent of OPEC output from one camp to the other. Moreover, Iraq gained control of revenue from Kuwait, which in fact served as an enclave for Western finance in the Arab world, since the Al-Sabah family accumulated most of its income in the West. The annexation was therefore both a 're-Arabization' of a significant proportion of oil revenue, and an extra point for the 'high price' camp.

However, all this was immediately thwarted by sanctions and a rise in Saudi oil production. After the outbreak of war (17 January 1991), oil prices stabilized at the 'Vienna July 1990' level, *without* Iraqi and Kuwaiti output, and despite a rather cold winter. Moreover, the military defeat of Iraq led to a significant price collapse. The truth is that the Western world did not need a little Kuwaiti discount merchant for it to get its surfeit of oil. Not in the short term, at least.

It was only very late in the day that President Bush gave the real clue, and confirmed the analysis of ecologists opposed to the war. On 19 February 1991, he revealed

United States energy plans for the following twenty years. Against every expectation, he called for a general acceleration of oil consumption and rejected a fuel tax, thus throwing retrospective light on his opposition to stabilization of CO_2 emissions at the World Conference on the Atmosphere held at Geneva in autumn 1990. The crucial concept was no longer flows but stocks; and by 2030, Saudi Arabia would have 40 per cent of proven reserves, and an Iraq–Kuwait bloc 30 per cent. All this, of course, on the assumption of a continuation of the 'energy-greedy' development model for which the United States is famous – their consumption of energy per dollar of GNP is twice as high as in Germany or Japan.

The Gulf War was therefore well and truly a war *for* oil, but *against* energy saving; *for* increased greenhouse effect and *against* the choice of a sustainable development model. In fact, at this rate (one which would give the Gulf countries a decisive role in crude oil markets in the run-up to the first quarter of the next century), the earth's average temperature will have risen by between two and four degrees – the extent of fluctuation of the glaciation cycle. However, whereas there were only a few million human beings at the time of the last climatic upheavals (stretching over tens of millennia), ten billion people over the next forty years will have to migrate to cope with climatic changes, in the context of a 'finite world' with increased racial tension.

This choice prompted a French diplomat to say 'United States energy policy is the Gulf War.' This can be understood in two ways: the Gulf War was the first step in a United States strategy to deal with the tense world which their energy policy (but not just theirs) implies. And this leads to the second theme in anti-warmonger interpretations of the second Gulf War – that it was a war for US hegemony.

The major change of the 1980s

At the G7 summit in Paris on 15 July 1989, it seemed that the 1980s were ending with the sorry failure of the 'socialist camp'. There was a new dawn over the world. The West magnanimously offered its hand to the Third World, and promised to lift the debt burden; already George Bush was making his generous gesture to the new 'Third World' to which the Second World was being reduced as the socialist gloss fell away. A few months later, the fall of the Berlin Wall completed the victory of the 'American camp'. In the same vein, Security Council resolutions after 2 August 1990 showed a single superpower orchestrating, in the name of a new international order, countries which calmly accepted its leadership. A few months later, the United States and some of its coalition partners (European or Arab) seemed to wage a private war of destruction, with the wary reproval of the then Soviet Union, Japan and most other European states (including some coalition members), and with cries of opposition heard in the streets of Arab capitals, a sign of a fresh wave of anti-Americanism in the Third World.

In fact, beneath the end of Cold War with the collapse of the 'Soviet camp', a completely new interpretation of the 1980s became possible. A mighty battle had been secretly going on right inside advanced capitalist countries, between the two options for countries to emerge from the Great Crisis of the 1970s. This battle – between 'liberal-productivism' and models based on 'negotiated involvement of workers' – has been the subject matter of this book. Moreover, we have already said that the big event of the end of the 1980s was the crushing victory of the second approach over the first – a victory judged, of course, on the criteria of capitalism: per capita GNP, profit margins, currency appreciation and, above all, trading surplus.

After 1985, the United States, despite a virtual 50 per cent devaluation against the yen and the mark, had a fairly regular trade deficit of $10 billion a month. By the early 1990s, its foreign debt was more than half that of the whole of the Third World. Moreover, like Brazil in the 1970s, this debt was self-sustaining. Disaster on the domestic front was even more spectacular – collapse of the loan system, education and health-care, an appalling social polarization between 'winners' and marginalized losers, an enormous increase in urban crime . . . and massive penetration by Japanese (and European) capital of key sectors of the American economy. This clear 'Brazilianisation' of the United States[12] has already happened in the United Kingdom. The fact that, in the early 1990s, France joined the camp of those countries with a deficit of industrial production, income polarization and 'inner-city violence' shows (allowing for time lag and other adjustments) where the wrong choice for 'restructuring' has inexorably led.

There is, however, a major counterpart to the American collapse – overwhelming military power. It has even been claimed that the level of defence spending in the 'liberal-productivist' countries (the United States, the United Kingdom, France), by diverting funds from civilian research, has led to their defeat by Germany and Japan, which were 'absolved' from paying for their own defence. In any event, it is a proven fact that defence spending has none of the knock-on effect promised for the civilian economy.[13] However, let us not mislead ourselves – American (and British and French) decline is not the result of military overspending, but of a more fundamental mistake in the way society deals with the relation between capital and labour. For me, the link between these two independent causes (excessive military spending, and wrong choices in recasting the capital–labour relationship) lies in the influence of the military hierarchical model on civilian work relations, and not directly in the wrong allocation of technological research. I would even go so far as to say (though with more circumspection) that the same was *also* true for the Soviet Union.

We still have this huge military machine, the only one in the world which can counter any geo-political threat, from any quarter. It constitutes the major advantage allowing the United States to maintain its position as the new century begins. 'To be top dog, keep Japan in check, break up Europe, and curb any Third World move for autonomy' is the frequent cry of anti-war people, but also of the most triumphalist of the pro-war camp. This is another statement which needs to be qualified and analysed more closely.

One particular paranoiac fantasy can be immediately discounted: that the United States, by controlling the Gulf, has a stranglehold over Germany and Japan. There will only ever be one single oil price on world markets, the same for American or Japanese imports. Experience showed that it was at the time of 'dear oil' (the period 1973–85) that Japan and Germany drew ahead of the United States, which is quite normal – when customers are rich, the most competitive exporters win out. Moreover, if (as their energy policy suggests) the United States, as masters of the Gulf (assuming they are!) impose cheap oil, this is hardly likely to worry Japan and Germany, which are now able to develop, outside OPEC, their own 'co-prosperity zones'.

There is a journalistic cliché which can also be discounted: that Germany and Japan are 'economic giants, but political pygmies'. Germany and Japan are not political pygmies – on the contrary, they operated remarkably skilfully in coping with the Gulf War. It is simply that their brand of *imperium* is not the same as that of the United States, or France, or Great Britain.

Reference has already been made to the German case. The reason why the Germans seemed to play, until

February 1991, a background role was that they were otherwise occupied – in absorbing and rebuilding a country of 18 million people, which Kohl's popularity-seeking policy of unification without transition had managed to ruin. The United States, on the other hand, was preparing for the much simpler task of destroying another country of the same size. Moreover, Germany had to keep an eye on its future zone of expansion, where the then USSR had been given a brief free run by Bush in return for its support in the Security Council. Neither could it cut itself off from the former Ottoman Empire, the southern flank of its traditional zone of influence, for which France was in theory responsible. An attempt will be made later to understand why France, as the 'European Ministry of African and Middle Eastern Affairs', failed to uphold the interests of Europe. Let us turn first, however, to Japan, where I was fortunate enough – and it was a very instructive experience – to spend half of the autumn in the lead-up to war.

In September and October 1990, the front page of the two Japanese English-language dailies covered three stories: the debate on the religious nature of the emperor's coronation, the Gulf War and the 'rice crisis'. The first of these served as a focus for all those, such as trade unionists, feminists and ecologists, who opposed the constitutional amendment proposed by Prime Minister Kaifu to allow Japanese military intervention in the Gulf. After a month of bitter conflict, the matter was settled in just two days when, in a way which was doubtless coordinated, all the countries of the future Japanese 'co-prosperity sphere' – South Korea, North Korea, both Chinas, Indonesia and Malaysia – declared that it would be 'unfortunate if Japan were to return to the international scene in the role of military power'. Immediately the bosses of the party in power (LDP) made it clear to Kaifu that it would be absurd to lose the friendship of our esteemed customers for such a trifling matter . . .

There remained the question of *financial* support for the war, and the 'rice crisis'. By this was meant the final US offensive to break through the wall of agricultural protectionism in the last phase of the Uruguay Round in the GATT trade talks. Japan, like South Korea and much more so than Europe, had in fact decided after the war to guarantee its self-sufficiency in food through comprehensive subsidies to small-scale agriculture. This system, which sets the price of rice in Japan at ten times the world level, guarantees the smallest rice grower a sizeable income – and any blue-collar worker can reconvert to rice growing. The result is that despite a notoriously low level of state welfare provision, Japan is a country almost as egalitarian as Sweden. This 'rice growers' welfare state' would have simply disappeared if Japan had given in to the demands of the Bush administration.

If we recall the situation in October 1990, it will be remembered that the US administration was then on the defensive, literally incapable of balancing the annual budget, and having to resort to the temporary lay-off of museum attendants and National Park rangers. However, by buying Federal Treasury bills, Japan made it possible for this bankrupt administration to make ends meet. There was a crying need to 'buy something' from the Americans, whereas Japan was much more competitive than the United States over the whole range of industrial production, apart from aeroplanes. This was when the Americans gave them the choice – buy American rice, or pay for an army to defend 'common interests' in the Gulf.

If one thinks hard about it, it was a hallucinatory situation. The former victor, former master of the world, was in the absurd position of a raw-material-exporting country trying to sell off its produce to pay for high-tech imports, or of barbarians laying siege to the Roman senate to get it to hire legions of mercenaries to defend the empire against other, more distant, barbarians, or, more accurately, of those pre-Renaissance Italian *condottieri*, hiring out Grand Companies of mercenaries to rich bourgeois cities to complement the local militia.

In December 1990, Japan decided not to allow the rice in, and to take the mercenaries as security. The result was the collapse of the Uruguay Round in GATT. In February 1991, it was announced that the money for the mercenaries ($9 billion) would be deducted from the Japanese Defence Force budget. Nothing had to affect the real weapons on which Japanese power was based – finance and technology.

Condottieri or policemen?

This therefore was the first way in which US military power was 'cashed in' – the enforced sale of mercenaries. And it was not insignificant: in fact, US military spending in the Gulf (estimated at $500 million a day) can be regarded as a straightforward export. Arms and personnel, with their munitions and canned meals, are American domestic produce (though the imports have to be deducted; one third of the electronics in US 'intelligent weapons' is said to use Japanese microchips). Since the cost of all this is paid for by foreigners, they are well and truly 'exports of goods and services', just like Boeing 747s sold to Japan, or the repatriation of money by Portuguese guest workers in Germany. The United States received $41 billion from their backers for the loan of this mercenary service (of which $9 billion came from Japan, $5 billion from Germany, $15 billion from Saudi Arabia and $12 billion from Kuwait). This paid for 80 days of military conflict, and, more importantly, for 5–8 months of trade deficit![14]

I am in no way saying, however, that the United States is planning to bring its foreign trade back into balance on a permanent basis by the enforced sale of mercenaries to countries in surplus. I am simply repeating that this kind of deal might in future be a significant item of annual revenue; and that if this is so, it is in the US interest for any tensions, in a world where these are increasing on the periphery of wealthier areas, to be solved by force rather than negotiation. I am also saying that, like any *condottiere* worried about the future, the United States will try to hire out armed forces for a *fixed payment* (by the year, and on a lease renewable by tacit agreement) to wealthy 'cities' which have no forces of their own.[15] I will even go so far as to say that it will try to make this role *official*, institutionalize it, and make sure it obtains a permanent hold over its 'customers' from this monopoly of legitimate violence. The US will try to become, not *condottieri*, but the world's policemen.

The two are not the same thing. A policeman is a public employee, on the permanent payroll. It is of course desirable, as far as the police budget is concerned, for crime to stay at a level which justifies the money set aside for it. More importantly, it is vital for the police always to observe the legal procedures which legitimate its carrying of weapons, for its actions to be within the law and the peacekeeping function as laid down by any legislature, and to be under the authority of an executive which allocates resources from a government budget.

This is why the United States attached so much importance to the United Nations and the Security Council during the first six months of the Gulf crisis, until Resolution 678 and even for a short time afterwards. The United Nations, the 'thingamajig' to which Reagan was reluctant to pay his dues only a short time before, came to be accepted as a kind of 'legislative body' responsible for approving the budget of the world's police force. 'Desert Shield' had to be seen as a proper police operation within the confines of the planet.

A *condottiere* is quite different: his job is to provoke

disorder in order to suppress it; he is a troubleshooter, virtually a racketeer, hand in glove with other *condottieri*, and with the Grand Companies of roving bandits who provide the need for his own services. It is disastrous for a mercenary when a robber band submits, or a gangster surrenders. This is why the Bush administration was in panic during the crazy week of 15–23 February 1991, when Saddam the bandit threatened to give in at the behest of the then Soviet Union, that former great power trying to get back into the centre of things by acting, with the inevitable intervention of Iran, as 'Ministry of the Humiliated and Dispossessed'. I have just indicated how such a surrender would have been 'disastrous', but that is not all: if Iraq, as the US military claimed, was about to collapse, there was nothing disastrous in letting its broken army return to a country in ruins . . . except for the *condottiere* whose job it was to attack it! That is why all serious reference in the Security Council to law, or the liberation of Kuwait, was dropped. Hired for 80 days, George Bush's Grand Company insisted on seeing the deal through.[16]

Condottiere or policeman: the two aspects of US power in the run-up to the twenty-first century will remain indistinguishable for a long time. The United States will always go for 'flat-rate work' alternating with limited-objective contracts; they will try continually to establish a style of international relations requiring resort to force, and they will always try, but always in vain, to legitimate and perpetuate this need. The 'general intifada' throughout the whole Arab world, indeed the whole Islamic world, which is what the 'victory of the West' in the second Gulf War could lead to, is therefore, in all possible cases, something the United States would welcome. The scene is even set for a third Gulf War – Turkey, Iran, Syria, the remains of Iraq, not forgetting the Kurds, Israel, and many more, and worse, and the US army is already in place. All it needs to do is choose its future employers, and enemies.

More serious is the question, the *only* question: how far can the United States in the end achieve geo-political domination from this vital role of *condottiere* or policeman? Certainly not world 'hegemony' – the undisputed management of world affairs, which they still had twenty years before. At the beginning of the twenty-first century, the world is firmly fixed in the *multipolar* mould.

We must be clear about this concept as well. The 'multipolar scenario' was conceived in the 1970s by those experts most aware of the incipient decline of the American empire. However, they were thinking of a purely geographical multipolarity – the United States had the American continent and the Middle East Europe had the Mediterranean and Africa, Japan had East Asia. The huge 'soft centre' of the world (the 'socialist' countries, already economically defeated, and the Indian subcontinent) would probably be fought over by a German-led Europe and Japan. This analysis is still valid, but another multipolarity has just been superimposed on it, this time a *functional* one, where Japan and Germany dominate in technology and trade terms (with some nice pickings for the US), and the United States dominates militarily. The question which interests us here is whether the 'world Ministry of Police' will not just pay the American '*condottiere*' for mercenary services, but will allow it to extend the boundaries of its geographical orbit, and even influence the rules of the game in world economic terms.

The Italian metaphor which has been used is not very illuminating. It is true that some Italian city-states fell under the temporary sway of an ambitious *condottiere*, a servant turned master; but by the end of the sixteenth century the major centres of the world economy – Pisa, Genoa, Florence and above all Venice – were controlled by capitalist elites; the Medici, rulers of Florence, were first and foremost bankers. More importantly, world order has always been established by economic powers like these. As Fernand Braudel said,[17] 'Taking the long view, only merchants count.' Even the essentially military power of the Spanish monarchy did not prevent it, and all its American colonies, falling to the forces of Genoa, Antwerp and Amsterdam.[18]

The lead-up to war had already, as we have seen, induced the Americans to give way to Japan and Europe over GATT. Of course, we must not rule out revenge scenarios – another round of trade talks where the Americans explicitly threaten to use force; but it is hard to see how American military superiority could be converted into economic advantage. It is easy to occupy Grenada or Panama, but less easy to crush Iraq, and it is unlikely that gunboat diplomacy could open up the Japanese rice market.[19] *Regionally*, however, there has been a clear extension of the American sphere. It may be that Arab markets are more amenable to American military exports, but they are not likely to be closed to Japanese or German non-military exports.[20] Moreover, through Turkey, the United States could drive a wedge between Europe and its south-western flank.[21]

Once again, it is probably from disruption in the South (as well as from the mega-Iraq that a disintegrating former Soviet Union could become) that the United States can expect to be given more 'contracts': sanctions against bad payers, 'execution' of assertive powers, and so on. This again is the policeman or the *condottiere*, and not really hegemony; neither is it the 'new international legal order'.

What about France?

In the new international regime, France operates only through the filter of its role in Europe. This, however, is not necessarily a weakness; it can be a source of strength.

Europe is in fact a microcosm of the world system, but better coordinated. Its major states retain a sphere of influence on a global scale, and this geographical multipolarity is matched by a functional multipolarity. Germany's role is that of Minister of Industry and Finance (so, *de facto*, that of prime minister), and France had the Ministry of the Third World, more particularly in respect of the Mediterranean, Africa and the Middle East. When François Mitterrand, on 24 September 1990, made his famous speech at the United Nations, which could have changed things considerably ('Iraq has only to announce withdrawal for everything to become possible . . . including an examination of the Palestinian question'), he clearly had the tacit and well-disposed support of Germany. How, therefore, could France move to a position of accepting Resolution 678, but then be absorbed totally in the American diplomatic and military set-up, to the point of a curt rejection of the Soviet plan and a commitment to a military thrust towards As-Salman?

The argument that 'Saddam rejected everything' does not hold water: the then Soviet Union managed to extricate itself in time from the diplomatic manoeuvring. The problem lies in France's shift of position, represented by opposition to the war on the part of its present and past ministers of foreign affairs and defence.

The primary reason seems to me to lie in the crisis of the Europe-system. Clearly, the Paris–Bonn 'lever' was countered, and spectacularly so, in the first week of January 1991, when two other EEC countries, Britain and the Netherlands, blocked any European approach which diverged from the American one. There are inherent reasons for this opposition to a Paris–Bonn axis – fear on the part of these two countries of a German-dominated Europe. But beyond this, the Amsterdam–London–Washington axis harks back to a much more significant historical trend; these are the three capitals of the 'capital-ist world-economy' (in the sense in which Immanuel Wallerstein and Fernand Braudel use the phrase). Not only have these three centres, in succession, governed the world, but they are also the home of the 'Seven Sisters' – the major oil companies which controlled the Middle East until 1973. The 'imperial culture' of these countries is radically different from the kind of hegemony sought by Germany and Japan. The Dutch and British empires were true colonial empires, sustained by a navy capable of military intervention. The United States divested itself of the need to occupy territory, but maintained a culture of direct military intervention. Although they were later on the scene, Germany and Japan also tried to establish empires, but these were dismantled – twice in the twentieth century in the case of Germany. After this bitter experi-ence, the two countries are going back to the Italian tra-dition of a disarmed empire – the straightforward capitalist domination of a 'co-prosperity sphere'.

As for France, and more particularly its social de-mocracy, it is imbued with the 'military' culture of the *imperium*. Suez and Algeria – two operations by govern-ments which included François Mitterrand – might have brought a cure. However, because of insufficient support by the EEC for an alternative policy, a long-standing reflex action could only induce France to fall in line with . . . Great Britain, so much so that it shared Anglo-Dutch fears of German power. Like Britain (and in the final analysis like the United States), France could try to bank on its military power and its Security Council membership to counter German economic hegemony. Moreover, as the third biggest arms exporter in the world, it could not go completely for a policy of negotiated disarmament by its customers. The contradiction was at its most acute because of the Gulf crisis, but the circumstances were such that the same reasons which made the United States act as *condottiere* to Germany and Japan led France to adopt the same attitude – because the French had *also* lost out in the economic war of the 1980s.

However, one cannot become a *condottiere* simply by wanting to be one. France received only $1 billion from Kuwait, and some loose change from Germany and Belgium (more perhaps than the real cost of joining the expedition, but less than the sum received by the British). Having therefore become merely another Britain, and having sacrificed priorities such as education and research to military spending, thus committing itself to its new role for the foreseeable future, France simply threw away, in the eyes of Arab opinion and present and future governments in the region, all the gains from the Gaullist policy of 'backing both horses'. Europe's Ministry for the Third World was left out in the cold.

For ever? Of course not. Just as Mitterrand sacked Defence Minister Chevènement because, as someone who preferred the other side of the contradiction, he was the wrong person to be Minister of Police, so Germany, momentarily shaken by France's desertion, began to look for a replacement 'Minister for the Third World'. There were plenty of candidates.

Straight after the 'massacre in the bunker' in Baghdad on 15 February 1991, Spain and Italy applied for the post by suggesting an end to the bombing of Iraqi civilian targets. But more importantly, Gorbachev rushed in to fill the vacant post. A very significant event was the direct telephone link between Chancellor Kohl and Gorbachev *during* the decisive talks which the latter was having with Tarik Aziz. In the hours which followed, Gorbachev tried to coordinate his approach with the Italians, and contacted President Mitterrand only on Saturday 23 February ('during lunch', as the latter noted in irritation), some hours before the slaughter. De Michelis was then able to put forward his plan to reform the Security Council, giving a seat to Germany, Japan and Italy – an old 'Axis' with, no doubt, a bright future.

The War of the Environment

The twenty-first century therefore begins against a back-cloth of North–South tension. A contradiction which overlies even the rivalries within the developed North: conflicts in the North are about relations with the South. It is not a matter of Manicheism: the South was represented in the Gulf War by the Saddam dictatorship, by the local imperialism of the Iraqi Baath. However, this North–South battle is part of a wider context of tensions, in which the North's responsibility is overwhelming.

To write a postscript to a conclusion in a changing world is not easy: one has to hope that it will not lose its relevance in the months after publication. However, I think I can say that the three years between the publication of the original French edition and this English translation in no way invalidated my analysis, and indeed provided significant confirmation of the validity of my proposals. I am even prepared to say that 1992 will be a spectacular illustration of what I have said in a vital area. It will mark the *first North–South battle in the global war of the environment*.

The threats to the planet which I denounced in Chapter 5 became a matter of common sense after the end of 1989. The martyrdom of Chico Mendes, the Amazonian peasant murdered by Brazilian landowners because he called for a 'sustainable' model for exploiting the tropical forest, was a significant influence in this increased awareness. We have seen the beginning of major diplomatic moves to establish a new world law of the environment, and the first boost to these efforts was the 1992 World Environment Conference in Rio de Janeiro.

I have made it very clear in this book that this new law

of the environment is absolutely vital. The fate of future generations depends on it. Enforcement measures, with penalties against breaches, are extremely urgent. Already, the more hyper-productivist countries of the South oppose such a move, explicitly condemning measures such as I suggested – the 'ecological and social clauses on free trade'. To these the Malaysian prime minister made this reply: 'Environment, democracy, human rights – these are the new obstacles which the developed countries want to put in the way of their future competitors.'[22] The dramatic thing is that the Gulf War, in identifying the idea of an international law with the principle of 'dual weights, dual measures', did not completely refute his statement.

When it comes to the greenhouse effect, for instance, it is clear that the increase of CO_2 in the atmosphere has to be stopped, and quickly. However, there are two ways of going about this.

The first method is to start from 'established rights', proposing the stabilization, then the reduction, of CO_2 emissions over the next thirty years, country by country. In this way, countries which have ravaged the biosphere for a hundred years and whose population is stable keep their 'share' of the world's right to pollute. Countries which have up to now been minimally responsible for the greenhouse effect, and whose population is rising rapidly, will have to share out the remainder. They are not allowed an industrial revolution.

The second approach starts with the idea of equality of rights for all human beings. It establishes a global annual pollution quota compatible with the regeneration capacity of the world ecosystem, and shares it between countries according to population. Each country is free to choose how to adapt to the quota, in return for a pooling of technology which restricts pollutant energy use. This is the way of autonomy and solidarity.

The first way implies that ecological imperialism still exists. The second implies a huge transfer of the 'right to pollute' from the North to the South, and a reform of development models which is much more restrictive for the North than for the South. The same argument is valid for the whole range of problems under discussion: protection of forests and biological diversity, and so on.

Bolstered by what they thought was a leadership crowned by the Gulf War, the United States' position in the Rio battle was one of radical eco-imperialism. As far as the greenhouse effect was concerned, they had already rejected (at the Autumn 1990 Geneva Conference) any 'precautionary principle', and on 19 January 1991, when the Gulf bombing was at its height, they reiterated that their development model was one based on oil. On bio-diversity, they made it abundantly clear that genes from virgin forests and farmers' fields were free of charge, whereas those from their own laboratories had to be paid for. However, they very soon came up against resistance. Countries of the South asserted their sovereignty, Europe and Japan challenged US hegemony by suggesting to the South a middle way, and powerful non-governmental organizations in the North (WWF, Greenpeace, Friends of the Earth) backed the ecologists and the popular movements of the South. Rio was a diplomatic Vietnam for the Bush Administration, since it was obliged to sign the Climate Convention (though it had managed to water it down significantly) and it was alone in its refusal to sign the Bio-diversity Convention, enshrining countries' right to their natural or traditional bio-diversity.

The twenty-first century began with a North–South war. It will continue with a battle fought by all humankind for the collective survival of the planet. To stop this battle of all humankind for itself turning once more into a North–South war, an alternative development is needed, in North and South. Its main elements will of necessity be akin to those put forward in this book. Today, choosing peace implies choosing a new, alternative, social and ecological model.

Notes

Preface

1 See my *Mirages and Miracles – The Crisis of Global Fordism* (Verso, London, 1988).

Chapter 1   The Fordist Compromise

1 Readers with an understanding of economics will find a more detailed analysis of Fordism and the crisis affecting it in my books *The Enchanted World – Money, Finance and the World Crisis* (Verso, London, 1985) and *Mirages and Miracles – The Crisis of Global Fordism* (Verso, London, 1988).
2 The French Fourth Republic lasted from 1946 to 1958, when an uprising in Algiers led to the return of General de Gaulle. The right held power for the first 23 years of the Fifth Republic.

Chapter 2   The End of the Golden Age

1 For an analysis of these interactions, see my *Mirages and Miracles – The Crisis of Global Fordism* (Verso, London, 1988).

Chapter 3   What Should Be Done?

1   The grasshopper and the ant appear in a La Fontaine fable, representing on the one hand a joyful and improvident approach to life, and on the other hand the virtues of providence.
2   'The free-running fox in the free-range chicken pen' is the definition of economic liberalism offered by Lamennais, a nineteenth-century Social Christian.

Chapter 4   The Impasses of Liberal-Productivism

1   The *Rassemblement pour la République* was the party of Jacques Chirac, French prime minister from 1986 until 1988, when he unsuccessfully stood as the right-wing candidate against the socialist François Mitterrand in the second round of the presidential elections.
2   Ideologue of liberal-productivism (the left-wing version) and critic of the welfare state.
3   Jargon used by French social welfare departments to describe adolescents from rundown urban areas, 'predestined' by their background to be delinquents.
4   Quoted by G. Santilli in his article '*L'automatisation comme forme de contrôle social*' (Automation as a Form of Social Control), *Travail*, 8, 1985.
5   P. Messine, *Les Saturniens* (La Découverte, Paris, 1987).
6   G. Wallraff, *Lowest of the Low* (Methuen, London, 1988); translation of *Ganz unten* (Kiepenhauer & Witsch, Cologne, 1985).
7   See M. Aoki, 'Intrafirm Mechanisms, Sharing and Employment', in S. Marglin and J. Schor (eds), *The Golden Age of Capitalism* (Oxford University Press, New York and London, 1990).

Chapter 7 Towards a New Wages Pact

1 Published as *Modernisation: Mode d'Emploi* (A Guide to Modernization) (UGE, Paris, 1987).
2 On the ambiguities of the Japanese model, see my article 'Fallacies and Open Issues of Post-Fordism', in A. Scott and M. Storper (eds), *Pathways to Industrialisation and Regional Development in the 1990s* (Routledge, London, 1992). I want once more to emphasize an obvious point – the real-world Japanese model cannot, any more than its mythological theorization called 'flexible specialization', be regarded as a socially progressist alternative, nor as the only technologically determined capitalist way. Any assimilation of the contentions in this part of the book with a eulogy of the Japanese model, or with the arguments of the English-speaking supporters of the 'New Times' and of 'flexible specialization', would therefore be totally wrong – see the very clear exposition by Richard Barbrook in 'Mistranslations: Lipietz in London and Paris', *Science as Culture*, No. 8, London, 1990.

On the other hand, in the face of criticisms (which I find excessive) of the over-optimistic analyses of the 'New Times', I maintain that the Japanese model is technically superior to the neo-Taylorism dominant in France and the English-speaking countries, and that, through the importance it gives to the intelligence of line operatives, it opens up the possibility (but *only* the possibility!) of future developments which are ecologically and socially progressist.
3 R. Mahon, 'From Fordism to?', *Economic and Industrial Democracy*, 8, 1987.
4 M. Cardoze, *Nouveau voyage à l'intérieur du P.C.F.* (Fayard, Paris, 1986).
5 Series of laws passed by the French left in 1982 to improve union rights and individual workers' rights of expression.

Chapter 8 *The Growth of Free Time*

1 Pierre Juquin had just left the Political Bureau of the French Communist Party. In the 1988 election, he was candidate against Antoine Waechter, the Green candidate, and was supported by Communist Party dissidents, odds and ends on the extreme left, and some feminists. He received 2 per cent of first-round votes, and Antoine Waechter received 4 per cent. In 1991, Juquin joined the Green Party.
2 The expression is used in M. Piore and C. Sabel, *The Second Industrial Divide* (Basic Books, New York, 1984).
3 Well-known French-owned holiday centres, where all facilities and activities are covered by a single lump-sum payment.

Chapter 9 *The Welfare Community*

1 The best criticism of the Fordist-type welfare state came not from libertarians, but from left-wing feminists. See S. Rowbotham, L. Segal and H. Wainwright, *Beyond the Fragments – Feminism and the Making of Socialism* (Allen & Unwin, London, 1981).
2 See the analysis in *Bulletin du Mauss*, 23, 1987.
3 See A. Lebaube, '*En marge du salariat*' (On the Fringe of the Wage-earning Class), *Le Monde*, 24 January 1989.
4 Rundown and crisis-ridden administrative area just outside Paris, where I headed an ecologist electoral list in the 1986 National Assembly elections.
5 Respected socialist educationalist and expert on the social and work integration of young people with problems.
6 In his preface to *L'Affaire de tous: initiatives locales et solidarité* (Everybody's Business: Local Initiatives and Solidarity), introduction by A. Lipietz (Syros, Paris, 1987).
7 Jack Russell, quoted by P. Messine, *Les Saturniens* (La Découverte, Paris, 1987).

Chapter 10 A Non-aggressive International Economic Order

1 C. Jedlicki, '*De l'impossibilité du remboursement de la dette à l'indispensable remboursement des banques*' (From Impossible Debt Repayment to Indispensable Bank Repayment), *Revue du Tiers Monde*, 99, 1984.

2 Between summer 1988 and summer 1989 there were many declarations and plans from governments such as France, Japan and the United States in favour of reducing Third World debt. The Paris Economic Summit on 15 and 16 July 1989 approved the Brady Plan, whereby banks would be urged to write off some of the debt owed to them, in return for a guarantee from the Big Seven on the remainder. This plan had only limited success, because once more the big capitalist countries were incapable even of providing a sufficient guarantee to make it attractive for private banks to reduce the debt owed to them. The only solution is a massive devalorization of debts together with partial repayment to the banks, but the latter is possible only if an international currency is created.

3 The 'Uruguay Round' of negotiations to reform the General Agreement on Tariffs and Trade, which had regulated international trade since the end of World War II.

4 D. Clerc, '*L'électricité la plus chère du monde*' (The Dearest Electricity in the World), *Alternative économique*, February 1988.

Chapter 11 The Alternative: A Project for Europe

1 Some historical dates: the Treaty of Rome, setting up the European Economic Community, was signed in 1957; de Gaulle was in power in France from 1958 to 1969; in 1981, the left came to power, but there was a right-wing government between 1986 and 1988; in 1985, EEC members signed the Single European Act which provided for the completion of a single market by 1 January 1993: the Single Act was

complemented by the Maastricht Treaty, signed in February 1992, and discussed in the Postscript.

2 The title of a book by M. Rocard et al. (Seuil, Paris, 1973).

3 Members of the *Fondation Saint-Simon*, including members of the anti-Marxist left (the 'second left'), particularly the editors of *Libération* and *Le Nouvel Observateur*, but also leaders of the CFDT trade union, and centrist businessmen such as Michel Albert and Alain Minc.

4 M. Albert and J. Boissonat, *Boom, crise, krach* (Boom, Crisis, Crash) (Seuil, Paris, 1988).

5 A. Minc, *La grande illusion* (The Great Illusion) (Grasset, Paris, 1988).

6 U. Zachert, '*Les formes d'emploi: problèmes et tendances actuelles en Allemagne fédérale*' (Forms of Employment: Current Problems and Trends in Federal Germany), *Colloque international sur les formes d'emploi*, November 1988.

7 Remember this was written in early 1989; that is, before German unification.

8 R. Musil, *Der Mann ohne Eigenschaften* (Hamburg, Rohwolt, 1930–52); translated as *The Man without Qualities* (London, Secker and Warburg, 1960).

9 J. Roth, *Radetskymarsch* (Cologne, Kiepenhauer and Witsch, 1979); translated as *The Radetsky March* (Harmondsworth, Penguin, 1984).

10 J. Roth, *Die Kapuzinergruft* (Cologne, Kiepenhauer and Witsch, 1972).

11 E. Terray, '*Pour une politique étrangère non munichoise*' (A Non-Munich Foreign Policy), *Les Temps modernes*, February 1989.

Postscript to the English Edition

1 See the two latest books by B. Coriat: *L'Atelier et le robot* (Robots in the Workshop) (Bourgois, Paris, 1990) and *Penser à l'envers – travail et organisation dans l'entreprise japonaise* (Turning Thinking on its Head – Work and Organization in Japanese Firms) (Bourgois, Paris, 1991).

2   See D. Leborgne and A. Lipietz, 'Fallacies and Open Issues of Post-Fordism' in T.F. Scott and N. Storper (eds), *Pathways to Industrialisation and Regional Development in the 1990s* (Routledge, London, 1992).

3   Institutional details: the European Community is a democratic monster. Its executive body is the *Commission*, whose members are appointed by member state governments. The Commission makes proposals to the *Council*, which is therefore the legislative body. The Council is composed of ministers from member state governments, so the European legislature is the sum of national governments! The directly elected European *Parliament* can only recommend, and the Council can ignore it. The Parliament can also force the resignation of the whole Commission, but this has never happened.

4   See D. Leborgne and A. Lipietz, 'Avoiding a Two-tier Europe', *Labour and Society*, 15, April 1990 (published by ILO, Geneva).

5   This racism later surfaced in the Gulf War, which a journalist on the main French television channel described as 'a clash between the civilized world and the Arabs'.

6   It goes without saying that the 'humanitarian' Security Council Resolution 688 was a useful reactivation of the 'right to interfere' in a state oppressing its own people. It is true that it was up to the Iraqi opposition to overthrow Saddam Hussein. The problem was that the United States, having given this opposition the signal to rise up, not only refused to give aid (just as they had done in the case of the Afghan opposition and the Nicaraguan Contras), but helped their oppressor.

7   'Apply the Resolutions on Palestine as strictly as the one on Kuwait' was the general call in France among supporters of Resolution 678. Let us be clear about this: it would be perfectly legitimate (and effective) to impose immediate trade and financial sanctions on Israel until Resolution 242 was fully complied with. The Palestinian state (of Resolution 181) does not even have to be set up, because in the consular sense it already exists (as does the neutrality of Jerusalem), and neither Egypt nor Jordan any longer claims Gaza and

the West Bank. But any future '678' threatening to bomb Israel out of existence within six months would encounter opposition which would be just as legitimate, and this time virtually unanimous; and I would be part of it!

8   This at least is the interpretation in P. Salinger and E. Laurent's book *Guerre du Golfe: le dossier secret* (Secret File on the Gulf War) (Orban, Paris, 1990). After the war, the American ambassador in Baghdad denied ABC network reports of her 25 July 1990 interview with Saddam Hussein, reproduced in the book. In it, she did in fact appear to give many 'green lights', and went so far as to assert that the Iraqi–Kuwait conflict 'did not concern the United States'. The denial was very late in the day, and all the less credible in that the whole world clearly heard President Bush, with the same consummate treachery, call on the Iraqi people to rise up, only subsequently to let it be crushed without lifting a finger, even giving Saddam back his helicopters.

9   It is to be noted at this point that Pakistan and Syria are almost equally good candidates for the next 'thrashing', from the point of view of 'potential threat'.

10   Z. Brzezinski, *'Une guerre ni nécessaire ni urgente'* (A War neither Necessary nor Urgent), *Revue Politique et Parlementaire*, December 1990.

11   The figures are for 1989, a 'normal' year. It goes without saying that, as it has shown since the war, Saudi Arabia can perfectly well supply a much bigger share of the market.

12   See A. Lipietz, *Mirages and Miracles – The Crisis of Global Fordism* (Verso, London, 1988).

13   See F. Chesnais, *Compétitivité internationale et dépenses militaires* (International Competitiveness and Military Spending) (Economica, Paris, 1990).

14   An important point is that the cost of a military expedition financed from abroad benefits the *government* which organizes it only by the difference between its real cost and the honorarium. On the other hand, for the exporting *nation*'s goods and services trading account, all of it has to be entered on the asset side, even if it is charged at cost price.

15   The Middle East 'security arrangements' under discussion in 1991 illustrate perfectly this 'fixed payment' trend:

- First (in the classic way, even though one might have hoped that the Iraqi lesson would have slowed the arms race), the United States sells some $15 billion' worth of arms to its allies in the Arab world.
- Then, it installs heavy and sophisticated weapons on a permanent basis in the small emirates . . . at the expense of the oil monarchies.
- Finally, Syria and Egypt supply infantry to defend these oil monarchies; with the money they receive, they buy grain from the United States.

16 For the reasons referred to above (to leave the Baath Party the means to keep order in Iraq), George Bush stopped General Schwartzkopf's offensive. The war therefore cost half as much as anticipated, and the providers of the money (Germany in particular) justifiably queried the estimate they had been given. At the time of writing, the United States have had only $7.2 billion from Japan, $7 billion from Kuwait, $6.9 billion from Saudi Arabia and $4.9 billion from Germany (figures given by Bob Hall, Pentagon spokesman, on 28 March 1991).

17 F. Braudel, *Le modèle italien* (The Italian Model) (Arthaud, Paris, 1989).

18 This argument was propounded by Paul Kennedy in the *Wall Street Journal*, 25 January 1991, in opposition to the Gulf expedition.

19 It is possible that Japan will open its rice market to the United States, not for military reasons but, again, for economic reasons – to find something to buy from the United States to balance their foreign trade!

20 The virtual monopoly which the United States seems to have achieved in the reconstruction of Kuwait should not mislead us: Kuwait was *already* in the American zone, and we must wait for the final figures.

21 Turkey, more than Iran, is the major regional victor. Denied membership of the European Community for the foreseeable future because of the Cyprus question and its peculiar interpretation of human rights, Turkey can hope for American support as it plans the rebuilding of its zone of influence.

This might be based on the whole Turkish-speaking or Muslim part of the disintegrating 'socialist' world, at the interface of Europe and Asia, from Bosnia to Uzbekistan. As we have already seen above, this is precisely the southern frontier zone of those countries 'not allowed into the EEC'.

22 Speech by Mohammed Mahathir given to the Asia Society, 4 March 1991.

Index